Contents

Autumn

Winter

Introduction

Learning through art can be a rewarding experience for children. Art is a tool through which they can express their creativity, use their imagination, and gain important insights. Working with art-related materials, concepts, and techniques helps enhance critical skills that children will use at many levels of their educational journey. For instance, art encourages the development of fine motor skills and eye-hand coordination. It teaches children to observe, listen, follow directions, analyze, and solve problems. By manipulating elements within an art activity, children learn about and apply their understanding of concepts such as shape, size, patterns, position, and spatial relationships. Just as importantly, art motivates and engages children, making it a perfect aid in teaching topics across all areas of the curriculum.

When you include art as an integral part of the curriculum, you provide children with hands-on, interactive experiences that can be used to introduce, reinforce, or enhance the concepts they need to learn. The multi-sensory aspects of creating art allow you to address different needs, strengths, and learning styles of your students. And, because art gives children a failure-free way to explore, create, and execute their own ideas, it helps build self-esteem and confidence.

The projects in *The Big Book of Quick & Easy Art Activities* are designed to connect art to seasonal topics that are typically taught in Kindergarten through third grade classrooms. In addition to teaching art methods and concepts, each project can be used to focus on skills related to a particular area of the curriculum, such as Math, Science, or Social Studies. To make every project more meaningful and extend its usefulness across the curriculum, a Language Arts link is provided to reinforce and give children practice in creative writing, phonics, word analysis, grammar, or other important literacy skill.

How to Use This Book

The Big Book of Quick & Easy Art Activities includes projects to use during every season of the year, reproducible patterns, and several pullout mini-charts and mini-posters.

Art Projects

The projects are organized by themes related to each of the four seasons: Autumn, Winter, Spring, and Summer. Each project is featured on a two-page spread and includes the following:

Curriculum Connection: This box at the top of the page names an area of the curriculum for which the project can be used. This is only a suggestion, and after reviewing the project, you might prefer to use it in connection with a different subject area, or more than one area. The key is to be flexible and use each project in a way that reinforces or enhances children's learning.

Title and Introduction: The title provides a brief description of the project and, in some cases, the art technique used to create it. Following the title is an introduction that suggests how the project might be used to address the subject area named in "Curriculum Connection."

Art Concepts: This section lists key elements of design, techniques, or other art concepts that can be taught during the activity. As children create, you'll likely discover additional art words and concepts that can be reinforced with the project. Feel free to include these as you introduce, explain, and model the procedures for making the project. A glossary of the art concepts listed for all the projects in the book can be found on pages 12–13.

Materials: The materials list is divided into several sections. The first section lists the visuals you need to display to introduce and demonstrate the project. The next section shows the materials each child will need to create the project. This is followed by a list of materials, if any, that can be shared by children. If the project requires an art station, such as for sponge painting or printmaking, there will be a final section that lists the supplies needed for that station.

Timesaving Tip: The tip provided in this section suggests a way in which you or children might save time in preparing for or constructing the project.

Let's Begin: This section provides a brief lesson plan that introduces the project and links it to the subject area identified in "Curriculum Connection" and the project introduction. Here, you'll also find a framework to follow as you guide children through an exploration and discussion of the project and related art concepts.

Step by Step: These easy step-by-step directions tell you how to construct the project.

One Step More: You'll find a suggestion for enhancing, displaying, or using the project in this section.

Language Arts Link: This section includes an activity that helps you target and teach a project-related literacy skill involving literature, writing, phonics, word analysis, vocabulary, or grammar.

Related Reading: You can refer to this list to find books that are related to the project. The selections might include fiction, nonfiction, or both. Share any or all of these books to extend the learning and enjoyment that children experience in making the project.

Reproducible Pages

Some projects in each section of the book call for the use of reproducible patterns. You can find these patterns on pages 168–196.

Mini-Charts and Mini-Posters

On pages 197–207, you'll find two reference mini-charts and four mini-posters that feature images of different artists' works. These handy resources can be pulled out and used as visuals for the projects that include them in the materials list.

A Word About the Language Arts Links

Literacy-teaching opportunities abound in all areas of an elementary curriculum, and art is no exception. The Language Arts Link for each project is designed to help you bridge the art activity to an important literacy skill and provide children with an activity that enhances and enriches their literacy development. You'll find that some links focus on early skills such as naming and writing letters of the alphabet, letter-sound correspondences, and syllable counts, while others target a range of skills related to phonics, phonemic awareness, word analysis, grammar, and vocabulary. In many activities, project-related words and concepts are used as springboards to introduce and reinforce specific skills, as well as to generate writing prompts. Children's books are suggested in several activities to connect projects with literacy skills. In the last part of each activity, an extension is provided for you to challenge more advanced children to perform higher-level skills. To further expand children's literacy experiences, you can choose from and share the books listed in Related Reading.

While doing these activities with children, you might be inspired to teach additional literacy skills or use a different approach to teach the targeted skill. Whether you choose to use the activity as described, adapt it, or expand the lesson, you'll discover that the development of children's literacy skills are just as much a work of art as are the projects in this book.

Helpful Hints

Preparing for the Activity

A few steps of preparation can help save time and prevent disasters. Following are some things you can do in preparation for each art activity:

✔ Plan the project setup and cleanup procedures ahead of time. On the day of the project, you can solicit children's help to do both. With an organized plan, a consistent routine, and a little direction, children can be very helpful in accomplishing these tasks quickly and effectively.

✔ In advance, gather all the supplies needed for the project, including the materials to display. When cutting paper to the specified sizes, cut a few extras to allow for mistakes children might make when creating the project.

✔ For a simple way to mount artwork, such as paintings, give children paper that has been trimmed ½- to 1-inch on each side. For example, you can cut a 12- by 18- inch paper to an 11- by 17-inch size. Then, children can glue their artwork onto the larger size sheet to create a border.

✔ Always construct the project yourself before presenting it to children. This will help you become familiar with the materials, procedures, and time it takes to make the projects, as well as to anticipate potential problems that might arise as children do the activity. While making the project, practice explaining the steps in ways that children can follow and understand. You can use your completed project as an example when you introduce the activity to children.

✔ In advance, prepare a place to put artwork that needs to dry. You might reserve an out-of-the-way area of floor space or set up a clothesline where children can hang their work with clothespins.

✔ You may want to distribute materials to children on an "as-needed" basis, especially if they are easily distracted or tend to be eager to begin or move ahead without waiting for directions.

✔ Before beginning a project, have children write their name on a paper or other material that will be used as a key piece of the project.

✔ If desired, plan to play music that is related to the activity or evokes a mood appropriate for the project.

Making Tagboard Templates

Often tagboard templates of a pattern are listed in the materials section. There are several ways you can make the templates:

✔ If your copy machine prints on tagboard, you can copy the patterns directly onto the number of tagboard sheets needed for the project and then cut them out.

✔ You can trace the pattern onto a sheet of tagboard, stack several more sheets behind it, and cut out the pattern through all layers. Cut out multiple copies of the pattern in this way until you have the number needed for the project.

✔ To create more durable templates, laminate the number of tagboard sheets needed for the project. Use a wipe-off pen to trace the pattern onto one tagboard sheet, stack several sheets behind it, and tape along the edges to hold the sheets together. Then, cut out the pattern through all layers.

Using the Mini-Charts and Mini-Posters

Prepare and use the convenient pullout mini-charts and mini-posters in the following ways:

✔ Gently remove the mini-charts and mini-posters from the book. If desired, back each one with a contrasting color of construction paper. Then, laminate them for durability. When not in use, store them in a file folder or between two sheets of tagboard.

✔ Use the color wheel mini-chart to reinforce color recognition, teach primary and secondary colors, cool and warm colors, and as a visual for children when working with complementary colors. Take time to explain how the color wheel is organized:

- Starting with yellow, every other color is a primary color.

- The colors between the primary colors are secondary colors.

- Warm colors are on the left side of the wheel, and cool colors are on the right.

- Each color is directly opposite its complementary color.

✔ Display the texture reference mini-chart to provide children with samples of texture designs. Children can refer to the chart to find designs resembling those in the visuals used to introduce the activity and to use in creating their own project.

✔ Use each art mini-poster when you present the project corresponding to that artist's work.

✔ Rather than storing the mini-charts, you might display them year-round in the art center. You can also display the mini-posters, either in the art center or in art-gallery fashion in another area of the room.

Sharing Materials

For many of the projects, children can share some materials. Here are a few ways to organize and make the materials easily accessible:

✔ Set out the materials in buffet-table fashion. You can sort craft items and smaller paper materials and place them in shoeboxes. Copy-paper box lids work well for larger paper. Be sure to label boxes that hold specific paper sizes needed for a project.

✔ Clean and use short peanut canisters to hold glue sticks, markers, crayons, craft sticks, and other similar materials.

✔ When finished using the materials, have children return glue sticks, crayons, and so on to the proper place.

✔ Keep a trash can handy so children can dispose of their discards as they work.

Setting Up Stations

Some projects list materials to use in sponge painting, printmaking, or other kinds of stations. Here are some tips for setting up and using stations:

✔ Place materials toward the middle of the table to give children plenty of workspace around the table edges. When deciding what size table to use, or how many, consider the materials children will be working with, how many children might use the station at one time, and how much workspace they need for the activity.

✔ For stations that include paint, be sure to keep paper towels on hand to clean up spills, splatters, and messy hands.

✔ Place several containers of water in the watercolor painting stations. When children want to change from one paint color to another, have them dip their paintbrush in water, wipe it on a paper towel, and then move on to the next color.

✔ Place paint smocks near the painting stations. Men's short-sleeved T-shirts or button-down shirts worn backwards work well to cover and protect children's clothing.

✔ For easy cleanup, cover painting station tables with newspaper. When the activity is over, just remove the paper and throw it away! You can put tempera paint on foam plates or trays and then toss them into the trash when finished.

✔ To clean paintbrushes, soak them for ten minutes in cool water with a little dishwashing soap. Then, rinse out the paintbrushes.

✔ Use foam plates or trays to hold gadgets and other items used for printmaking.

Drawing Pictures

Many of the projects require children to draw, whether it's tracing a template, drawing a shape, or creating a scene. Try these tips to help children experience success in the steps that include drawing:

✔ Have children always trace the tagboard templates in pencil.

✔ Before drawing in pencil, ask children to finger-draw specific shapes for the project in the air or on paper. This step helps save time, paper, and erasers, and lets you check for understanding and offer help to work out potential problems.

✔ To practice drawing more complex pictures, children can use a pencil eraser to "sketch" out the picture and then trace it with pencil. Have children make pencil-drawings of any shapes or pictures before coloring them.

✔ For many projects, the step-by-step "look and draw" technique works well. With this method, you can model each step as you guide children through the drawing process. While demonstrating, draw a few lines at a time as children observe. Then, give them time to follow your example. The object is not to have children make an exact replica of your drawing but rather to help them succeed in executing the activity. This method is especially useful in helping children position objects in particular places on their paper.

✔ When modeling drawing steps, be sure to position yourself and the materials so that children have a clear view of what you're doing. Work at a pace that allows children to keep up with you.

✔ No matter how simple or complex the drawing task, encourage children to always try. Also look for ways to encourage their originality and help them express their ideas.

Basic Materials and Equipment

For each activity, you'll find a complete list of the materials needed to make the project. The following includes common supplies children will use in many of the projects, as well as equipment that will come in handy as you prepare for making or displaying the projects.

- Colored construction paper in two sizes: 9- by 12-inch and 12- by 18-inch
- Pencils, erasers, fine-tip black permanent markers, crayons, color markers, and oil pastels
- Glue sticks, white glue, tape, and staplers
- Scissors and hole punches
- Rulers
- Tempera paint in assorted colors
- Paintbrushes in assorted sizes, including foam brushes
- Watercolor paint sets or watercolor cubes in individual colors
- Sponges cut into 1-inch squares
- Plastic thread spools, soda bottle caps, foam peanuts, and other assorted gadgets for printmaking
- Foam plates or trays to put paint in
- Containers for holding paint and water
- Newspaper and paper towels
- Paper cutter
- Laminator

Glossary of Art Terms

alternating pattern: a pattern in which every other element is identical (example: circle, square, circle, square, and so on)

background: the part of a scene or picture that appears to be distant and far from the viewer

collage: work of art made of various materials (such as paper, cloth, or wood) glued onto a surface

color: a particular wavelength of light reflected by an object, usually determined visually by its hue, value, and intensity (and referred to by its hue name: red, orange, yellow, green, blue, or violet/purple

complementary colors: two colors that are opposite each other on a color wheel, with one being a primary color and the other a secondary color (such as red and green)

contrasting colors: two colors that differ in darkness and lightness

cool color: a color that represents coolness, such as blue, green, or purple

crayon resist: the process of applying wax-based crayon to paper so that when water-based paint is applied, it colors only the paper and is resisted by the wax from the crayons

foreground: the part of a scene or picture that appears nearest and in front of the viewer

form: the three-dimensional shape and structure of an object

horizon: the line that forms the apparent boundary between the earth and sky as seen by an observer

landscape: a natural scene (such as mountains, a field, and so on)

line: a continuous mark or stroke—straight, curvy, or angular—made by a pen, pencil, or brush on a surface

mosaic: a picture or design made by putting together small pieces of colored material (such as paper or tile)

negative space: the area surrounding a two or three-dimensional shape (see positive space)

origami: a Japanese art form in which squares of paper are folded to represent objects

overlapping: an art method in which an object partially covers another object to give the appearance of depth

pattern: the repetition of one or more design elements, such as line, shape or color

positive space: the area occupied by a two-dimensional or three-dimensional shape (see negative space)

primary colors: the three colors—red, yellow, and blue—on a color wheel from which all other colors are created

printmaking: an art technique in which an impression of an object (such as a sponge or thread spool) is transferred onto paper or another material

profile: the outline of the side view of a head or face

radial: a ray-like arrangement of design elements around a central point

secondary colors: the colors—green, orange, and purple—on a color wheel that are made by mixing two of the three primary colors

shape: a line that crosses back upon itself and encloses a space

silhouette: an outline of an object that is filled in with a solid color, such as black

skyline: an outline, such as buildings or mountains, against the background of the sky

symmetry: the visual balance of an object or picture when both sides of a centerline match in color, line, and shape to produce a mirror image

tessellation: a pattern made up of designs that fit together and repeat over and over

tactile texture: the actual feel of a surface's texture (such as rough or furry)

three-dimensional: an object that has width, height, and depth, making it appear more realistic (can also be called form)

two-dimensional: an object that has only width and height, such as paper (can also be called shape)

visual texture: the illusion or appearance of a surface's texture

warm color: a color that suggests warmth, such as red, yellow, or orange

Meeting the Language Arts Standards

The "Language Arts Link" activities are designed to support you in meeting the following standards for children in grades K-3, outlined by Mid-Continent Research for Education and Learning (McREL), an organization that collects and synthesizes national and state preK-12 curriculum standards and suggests what teachers should provide for their students to grow proficient in language arts, among other curriculum areas.

Uses the general skills and strategies of the writing process:

- Uses writing and other methods (e.g., using letters or phonetically spelled words, telling, dictating, making lists) to describe familiar persons, places, objects, or experiences

- Writes in a variety of forms or genres (e.g., picture books, stories, poems, personal experience narratives, responses to literature)

- Writes for different purposes (e.g., to entertain, inform, learn, communicate ideas)

- Uses the stylistic and rhetorical aspects of writing

- Uses descriptive words to convey basic ideas

- Uses grammatical and mechanical conventions in written compositions

- Uses complete sentences in written compositions

- Uses nouns in written compositions (e.g., nouns for simple objects, family members, community workers, and categories)

- Uses verbs in written compositions (e.g., verbs for a variety of situations, action words)

- Uses adjectives in written compositions (e.g., uses descriptive words)

- Uses conventions of spelling in written compositions (e.g., spells high frequency, commonly misspelled words from appropriate grade-level list; spells phonetically regular words; uses letter-sound relationships; spells basic short vowel, long vowel, r-controlled, and consonant blend patterns)

Uses the general skills and strategies of the reading process:

- Uses mental images based on pictures and print to aid in comprehension of text

- Uses basic elements of phonetic analysis (e.g., common letter/sound relationships, beginning and ending consonants, vowel sounds, blends, word patterns) to decode unknown words

- Uses basic elements of structural analysis (e.g., syllables, compound words, spelling patterns) to decode unknown words

- Understands level-appropriate sight words and vocabulary (e.g., words for persons, places, things; high frequency words)

Uses listening and speaking strategies for different purposes:

- Makes contributions in class and group discussions (e.g., reports on ideas and personal knowledge about a topic, connects ideas and experiences with those of others)

- Responds to questions in class (e.g., gives reasons in support of opinions, responds to others' ideas)

- Uses level-appropriate vocabulary in speech (e.g., words that describe things, events, locations, actions; synonyms, antonyms, homonyms)

- Gives and responds to oral directions

Source: *Content Knowledge: A Compendium of Standards and Benchmarks for PreK-12 Education*, (4th edition). (Mid-Continent Regional Educational Laboratory, 2004)

Shapely School Bus

Use these personalized school buses as a springboard to review bus safety rules and routines.

Art Concepts
shape
color
pattern

Materials

To display:
- pictures of school buses
- completed project

For each child:
- 9- by 12-inch yellow construction paper
- pencil
- scissors
- four 2-inch squares of white construction paper
- 1- by 4-inch white construction paper
- two 3-inch squares of black construction paper
- 2-inch square of red construction paper

To share:
- 12 tagboard school bus templates (page 168)
- fine-tip black permanent markers
- color markers or crayons
- glue sticks
- scraps of colored paper

Let's Begin

Ask children to examine the bus pictures and completed project and tell what colors and shapes they see. Are there any repeating shapes, colors, or lines on the buses? Point out the row of windows divided by the yellow bus frame and the black lines that run across the sides of the buses. Tell children that these are examples of a pattern. Explain that a pattern is formed by repeated lines, shapes, or colors.

Inform children that they will create a school bus using the colors, shapes, and patterns featured on an actual school bus. Pass out the materials and demonstrate the procedures as children follow along.

Timesaving Tip!

Use a paper cutter to cut the white, black, and red construction paper into the sizes needed for the project. You can stack and cut several sheets at a time.

Step by Step

1. Use a pencil to trace the school bus template on the yellow paper. Cut out the shape.

2. Draw a bus driver on one 2-inch square of white paper, yourself on another white square, and a different friend on each additional white square. Draw a bus door on the 1- by 4-inch white rectangle. Trace each drawing with the black marker. Then, color each picture as desired.

3. Glue the driver's window, door, and other bus windows onto the bus, leaving a space between each piece.

4. For wheels, cut out a circle as large as possible from each black square. Glue one wheel near the front end of the bus and the other wheel near the back end.

Cut out wheels.

5. Cut out a stop sign from the red square. Write "Stop" on the shape and glue it below the driver's window.

6. Draw several thick black parallel lines across the side of the bus. Write "School Bus" between the two top lines.

7. Cut out other details from scrap paper and glue these onto the bus.

One Step More

For an interesting border, display the buses bumper-to-bumper across the top edge of a wall or around a bulletin board or door frame.

Language Arts Link

Ask children to imagine they're riding a bus on a class trip. Have them name the things they see and experience that begin with B (such as bumpy roads, bugs, billboards, and so on). List their responses on chart paper and then read each B word with the class. More advanced children might write about their imaginary trip, using as many B words as possible.

Related Reading

The Bus for Us by Suzanne Bloom (Boyds Mill Press, 2001)

The Little School Bus by Carol Roth (North-South, 2004)

School Bus by Donald Crews (Greenwillow, 1984)

The Smushy Bus by Leslie Helakoski (Millbrook Press, 2002)

Silhouette Symmetry

These silhouettes make a great discussion starter about ways children can appreciate and accept themselves and others.

Art Concepts

silhouette
profile
symmetry
printmaking

Materials

To display:
- various examples of silhouettes
- completed project

For each child:
- 9-inch square of black construction paper
- scissors
- 10-inch square of white construction paper
- 12-inch square of gray construction paper

To share:
- white chalk
- glue sticks

For printmaking station:
- shallow trays of tempera paint in various colors
- objects for printing (spools, wood blocks, and cut sponges)

Let's Begin

Examine with children the silhouettes and completed project. Tell them a silhouette is an outline of an object that is filled in with a solid color, such as black. Ask them to tell what the silhouettes in the completed project represent. Explain that the two silhouettes are a profile, or the side view, of a person. They're also symmetrical because the silhouettes are the same on both sides of the project. Finally, point out that the border on the project was created by making paint prints of a common object.

Tell children that they will use their own silhouettes to create a symmetrical picture. Pass out the materials, pair up children, and explain that their partners will draw their silhouettes for them. Then, demonstrate the procedures as children follow along. (Note: For safety reasons, be sure to supervise children closely during Step 2.)

Timesaving Tip!

Set up your printmaking station ahead of time. Cover a table with newspaper and place the printmaking objects on it. Add the trays of paint just before beginning the activity.

Step by Step

1. Fold the black paper in half. Place the paper on the table with the folded side on your right. Then, turn your head to the right and gently lay it on the paper with the top of your head near the top of the paper and your nose near the fold. Your partner can help adjust the paper as needed.

2. When the paper is in place, remain quiet and still—with eyes and mouth closed— while your partner slowly and carefully draws your profile with chalk. To do this, your partner will trace along the outline of your head from the top to the bottom of the paper, keeping the chalk about ½-inch away from your head so that it doesn't rub against you.

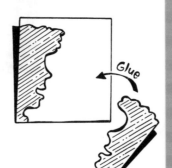

Trace the profile.

3. Cut out your profile, keeping the paper folded. When finished, you'll have two silhouette cutouts of your profile. Place the straight side of one cutout along the left edge of the white square, and glue it down. Flip the other cutout and glue it along the right edge of the paper. The profiles will be facing each other.

Glue

4. Glue the white paper to the center of the gray paper.

5. To frame your silhouettes, take the project to the printmaking station. Choose one or more printmaking objects to make paint prints around the edges of the gray paper.

One Step More

Create a bulletin board to highlight the concept of symmetry. Use the projects as the centerpiece for the display.

Language Arts Link

Invite children to dictate sentences about things they would like their classmates to know about them. Write their dictation on speech bubble cutouts. More advanced children can write their own sentences on the speech bubbles. Display children's speech bubbles with their projects.

Related Reading

I Like Being Me: Poems for Children, About Feeling Special, Appreciating Others, and Getting Along by Judy Lalli (Free Spirit Publishing, 1997)

I Like Myself! by Karen Beaumont (Harcourt, 2004)

I'm Gonna Like Me: Letting Off a Little Self-Esteem by Jamie Lee Curtis (Joanna Cotler, 2002)

It Looked Like Spilt Milk by Charles G. Shaw (HarperTrophy, 1988)

Mosaic Monograms

*As children share these colorful monograms with the class,
invite them also to share things that make them unique individuals.*

Art Concepts

primary colors
secondary colors
complementary colors
mosaic

Materials

To display:
- color wheel (page 197)
- completed project

For each child:
- 9-inch square of black construction paper
- white chalk
- glue stick

To share:
- 1-inch squares of red, yellow, blue, orange, green, and purple paper (each color in a separate box)

Let's Begin

Display the color wheel and ask children to name the six colors on it. Point out the primary colors: red, yellow, and blue. Inform children that the other three colors (orange, green, and purple) are secondary colors because they are made by mixing together two primary colors. Continue by pointing out the two colors directly opposite each other on the color wheel: red and green, blue and orange, and yellow and purple. Explain that these are called complementary colors. Then, have children examine the completed project. What was used to fill in the letter and background? (small squares of paper) Tell them that this art form is called a mosaic.

Let children know that they will make a mosaic using one of their initials, sometimes called a monogram. Pass out the materials and demonstrate the procedures as children follow along.

Timesaving Tip!

Keep a supply of moist paper towels on hand for children to use to wipe glue off their fingers. This will prevent frequent trips to the sink to wash hands.

Step by Step

1. Using chalk on the black square, draw the initial for your first or last name in the form of a block letter. Be sure to draw the letter large enough so that it fills up the black square from top to bottom and is at least 1-inch wide.

2. Choose a pair of complementary colors (red and green, blue and orange, or yellow and purple). Decide which one of the two colors you want to use for the background and which one to use for your initial. Once you decide, glue paper squares in the selected color onto the area surrounding your initial. Glue the squares close together, overlapping them as needed, to cover the black paper.

3. Glue squares in the other color onto your block initial, making sure you cover the black paper as completely as possible.

One Step More

Mount the projects on 12-inch squares of colored construction paper for displaying. If the background for the initial is a secondary color, choose a primary color for mounting. Conversely, if the background is a primary color, mount the project on paper in a secondary color.

Language Arts Link

Ask children to describe themselves using words that begin with the same letters as their initials (or the letters of their name). Have them list their words on paper and then share the list with the class. More advanced children might write a poem about themselves, starting each line with a word that begins with a letter in their initial or name.

Related Reading

A, My Name is Alice by Jane E. Bayer (Puffin, 1992)

Chrysanthemum by Kevin Henkes (Greenwillow, 1991)

My Name Is Yoon by Helen Recorvits (Farrar, Straus and Giroux, 2003)

The Turn-Around, Upside-Down Alphabet Book by Lisa Campbell Ernst (Simon & Schuster, 2004)

Paper Bag Houses

*Invite children to use these 3-D houses to share information
about themselves and their homes with classmates.*

Art Concepts

shape
texture
three-dimensional

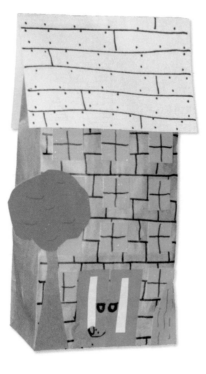

Materials

To display:

- pictures of different kinds of homes (houses, apartment buildings, mobile homes, and so on)
- texture reference chart (page 199)
- completed project

For each child:

- brown paper lunch bag
- color markers
- scissors
- glue stick
- newspaper
- 6- by 8-inch construction paper (tan, gray, or brown)

To share:

- scraps of colored paper
- tape

Let's Begin

Encourage children to describe the different shapes and designs found on the pictured homes, as well as on their own homes and other homes they have seen.

Have them also talk about how the materials used on the outside of homes look (such as wood, brick, and stone). Ask children to refer to the texture reference chart to find designs that might resemble the appearance, or texture, of these materials. Then, show them the completed project and have them identify the different shapes, designs, and textures found on it. Explain that the paper bag house differs from the pictures of homes because it has three-dimensions— height, width, and depth.

Tell children that they will design a three-dimensional paper bag house to represent their own home or an imaginary home. Pass out the materials and demonstrate the procedures as children follow along.

Timesaving Tip!

Precut squares and rectangles in different sizes and colors for children to use for the doors, windows, and shutters on their houses.

Step by Step

1. Refer to the texture reference chart to find a design that most resembles the kind of material you'd like to have on the outside of your house. Or create your own design and practice drawing it on a piece of scrap paper. Once you decide on a texture for the outside of the house, use markers to draw the design on each side of the bag.

2. Draw windows, doors, shutters, a chimney, and other house details on colored scrap paper. Cut out each item and glue it onto the house.

3. Open the bag and fill it with crumpled sheets of newspaper. Tape the top edges of the bag together.

4. To make a roof, fold the 6- by 8-inch paper in half. Use a marker to draw a shingle design on both sides of the folded paper. Then, place the roof over the top of the bag and glue each side in place.

One Step More

To make their paper bag houses feel more like home, add cutouts of bushes, flowers, outdoor furniture, pets, and so on.

Language Arts Link

Ask children to draw a picture of a room in their house. Have them write the names of objects found in their pictures, such as a chair, shelf, or rug. As children share their drawings with the class, tell them that the names of the objects in their pictures are nouns. More advanced children might write sentences to describe a room in their house and then underline all the nouns in their sentences.

Related Reading

Houses and Homes (Around the World Series) by Ann Morris (HarperTrophy, 1995)

My House by Lisa Desimini (Henry Holt & Company, 1994)

Community Skylines

Use these unique skylines to focus children's attention on the buildings, community workers, and activities in their community.

Art Concepts

shape
contrasting colors
overlap

Materials

To display:

- pictures of skylines representing cities, small towns, neighborhoods, and other types of communities (include day and night skylines)
- completed project

For each child:

- 9- by 12-inch black or blue construction paper
- pencil
- scissors
- fine-tip black permanent marker
- glue stick

To share:

- scraps of colored paper

Let's Begin

Display the completed project and skyline pictures. Have children describe the shapes they see on the buildings. Point out how the roofs and other structures, such as flags, satellite dishes, and church steeples, create interesting shapes against the sky. Explain that when dark and light colors are put together, they are called contrasting colors. Do children see any contrasting colors in the display items? Have them also look for examples in which a building or object overlaps, or partially covers, another building or object.

Tell children that they will create a community skyline to represent buildings or structures in their community. They might create a skyline of an actual scene (such as a row of city skyscrapers or a small town) or one that includes a combination of interesting structures, such as a home with an unusual roofline, a business with a large mascot on its roof, and a public statue. Pass out the materials and demonstrate the procedures as children follow along.

Timesaving Tip!

Enlist a volunteer to sort the paper scraps, placing the light colors in one box and the dark colors in another.

Step by Step

1. To make a day skyline, use a blue sheet of 9- by 12-inch construction paper for the background. Use black paper for a night skyline. Keep this sheet of paper handy to use as a reference for determining the size and shape of the buildings and structures to include in the skyline.

2. Choose paper scraps in different sizes, shapes, and contrasting colors to use for the buildings or structures you plan to use in the skyline. Use a pencil to draw the building or structure and then cut out each shape. Use a black marker to add details, such as doors and windows, to each cutout.

3. Arrange all the cutouts on the background, placing them so that they touch and overlap and contrasting colors are side-by-side. After placing all the cutouts where you want them, glue them onto the background.

One Step More

To give the skyline more contrast, use oil pastels or glitter glue to create additional details on the buildings and structures.

Language Arts Link

Invite children to use the same technique to create word skylines. Have them choose a word, cut out the shape for each letter in the word, and then arrange the letters to form a word skyline. They can add details as desired. More advanced children might create and sequence their word skylines to make complete sentences.

Related Reading

The Alphabet Tree by Leo Lionni (Knopf Books for Young Readers, 2004)

Community Helpers from A to Z by Bobbie Kalman (Crabtree Publishing Company, 1997)

A Good Night Walk by Elisha Cooper (Orchard Books, 2005)

On the Town: A Community Adventure by Judith Caseley (Greenwillow, 2002)

Mini Letter Banners

Interesting designs add an element of fun when children use these mini banners to practice their letter knowledge.

Art Concepts

shape
line
pattern
texture

Materials

To display:

- completed banner featuring at least one of each shape: square, circle, and triangle
- texture reference chart (page 199)

For each child:

- 9- by 12-inch blue construction paper
- pencil
- fine-tip black permanent marker
- oil pastels

To share:

- tagboard template for each letter, enlarged by 150% (pages 169–170)
- 10 tagboard templates for each shape: square, circle, and triangle (page 171)
- 12- by 15-inch construction paper in bright colors
- glue sticks

Let's Begin

Ask children to examine the banner and name the shapes they see. Have them identify the letter in each shape. Then, have them look at the designs that surround and fill in the open areas of the letters. Explain that each design is made up of a series of repeating lines that create a pattern. Point to and name the kind of lines used to create each pattern, such as horizontal, vertical, diagonal, curvy, or zigzag lines. Help children locate the different lines on the texture reference chart. Encourage them to share their thoughts on what kinds of textures the lines might represent. For example, curvy lines might give the appearance of a bumpy texture while straight lines indicate a smooth texture.

Tell children that they will create a mini letter banner to use in letter recognition activities. Pass out the materials and demonstrate the procedures as children follow along.

Timesaving Tip!

For quick and easy letter templates, use a die-cutter to cut 2½-inch letters from tagboard.

Step by Step

1. Choose six letter templates. Examine the shape of each letter and decide whether it fits best on a square, circle, or triangle template. For example, *G* fits best in a circle, *H* in a square, and *A* in a triangle. Use a pencil to trace the selected shape for each letter onto the blue construction paper. Then, trace the letter onto the shape. (More advanced children might draw freehand block letters.) Using the black marker, trace the lines for each shape and letter.

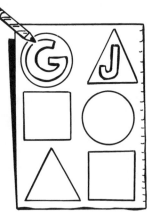

2. Pencil in a repeating line pattern in the area around each letter, staying within the border of the shape. You can refer to the texture reference chart for inspiration on the kinds of lines to use. Use a different line pattern around each letter.

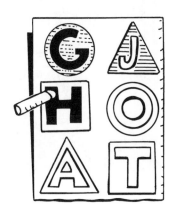

3. Use oil pastels in different colors to color in the letters and trace the line patterns. To avoid smearing the colored parts of the page, work from left to right and top to bottom.

4. To create a banner, glue the letters onto a 12- by 15-inch sheet of bright-colored construction paper.

One Step More

To create a class letter banner, mount the mini banners onto a length of bulletin board paper. Then, display the banner in a prominent place so you can use it for letter-related activities.

Language Arts Link

Name a letter and have children find it on the banners. Invite them to brainstorm words that begin with the sound that letter represents. For a more advanced activity, point to one letter at a time to spell out a word, such as C-A-T. Have children sound out the letters and say the word (they might write the letters on paper first).

Related Reading

A, My Name Is Alice by Jane E. Bayer (Puffin, 1992)

Chicka Chicka Boom Boom by Bill Martin, Jr. and John Archambault (Simon & Schuster Books for Young Readers, 1989)

Old Black Fly by Jim Aylesworth (Henry Holt and Co., 1992)

Crayon-Resist Pattern Blocks

Reinforce counting, addition, and multiplication with the shape patterns featured on these colorful projects.

Art Concepts

shape
color
pattern
crayon resist

Materials

To display:
- completed project

For each child:
- 9- by 12-inch white construction paper
- pencil
- fine-tip black permanent marker

To share:
- fluorescent crayons

For watercolor paint station:
- red and yellow watercolor paints
- wide or chubby paintbrushes
- containers of water

Let's Begin

Have children examine the completed project. What colors and shapes do they see? Explain that a pattern is created when one or more elements, such as color and shape, are repeated. Point out one block on the project at a time. Do children see a color or shape pattern on the block? Afterward, tell children that this project was made using a technique called "crayon resist." First, the shapes were colored with crayons and then painted with watercolor paint. The paper surrounding the shapes absorbed the paint, but the crayon on the shapes resisted the paint and pushed it away.

Tell children that they will create four pattern blocks on a sheet of paper using the crayon resist technique. Pass out the materials. and demonstrate the procedures as children follow along.

Timesaving Tip!

Set up the watercolor paint station ahead of time. Cover a table with newspaper and place the watercolors, water containers, and paintbrushes on it. You might cover all the colors in the paint tray except red and yellow with masking tape.

Step by Step

1. Fold the 9- by 12-inch white paper in half. Then, fold it in half again. Unfold the paper to reveal four sections divided by the fold lines.

2. Starting in one section of the paper, draw a row of shapes in pencil. You might use the same shape across the row, or use a repeating pattern of two different shapes. Continue to draw identical rows of the pattern until you fill in that section of the paper. Then, trace each shape with the black permanent marker.

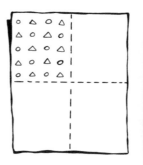

3. Choose two fluorescent crayons in different colors. Use them to color the shapes in your pattern. If the pattern has only one shape, color every other shape a different color. If the pattern has two shapes, use one color for one type of shape, and the other color for the other shape. Press firmly and be sure to color each shape as completely as possible.

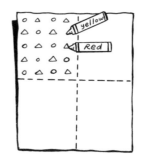

4. Repeat Steps 2 and 3 for the other three sections of the paper. Use a different pattern and color scheme for each section.

5. Take the project to the watercolor paint station. Apply a wash of red watercolor paint to one section of patterns and then to the section on the opposite corner of the page. Paint a yellow watercolor wash over the remaining two sections. As you paint, notice how the crayon pushes away the paint and makes the colored patterns look brighter.

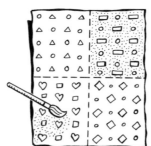

(Note: More advanced children might use three or more shapes and colors in their projects.)

One Step More

After the project dries, glue it to a 12- by 18-inch sheet of dark blue or white construction paper for displaying.

Language Arts Link

Share a story containing repetitive text (see Related Reading). Then, explain that, like the shapes and colors in their projects, the events in the story follow a pattern. Reread the story, inviting children to read along each time you come to a repeated part. More advanced children can write their own stories using a repetitive text pattern similar to that in the story.

Related Reading

Brown Bear, Brown Bear, What Do You See? by Bill Martin, Jr. (Henry Holt and Company, 1996)

The Doorbell Rang by Pat Hutchins (Greenwillow, 1986)

Jump, Frog, Jump! by Robert Kalan (HarperTrophy, 1989)

The Napping House by Audrey Wood (Harcourt, 1984)

Apple Overlaps

These eye-catching projects will add delicious color to children's explorations of apples from tiny seed to yummy fruit.

Art Concepts

overlap
color
crayon resist

Materials

To display:
- three apples, each a different color (red, green, and yellow)
- completed project

For each child:
- 12- by 18-inch white construction paper
- pencil

To share:
- black, red, green, yellow, and brown crayons

For watercolor paint station:
- blue and purple watercolor paints
- wide or chubby paintbrushes
- containers of water

Let's Begin

Place the apples on a table so that from the class's view, one or two apples are partially covered by another apple. Ask children to name the apple colors and describe what they see. As they share, help them understand that the apples appear to overlap each other. Explain that artists use overlapping to make their work look more realistic. Then, draw children's attention to the overlapping apples in the completed project. Point out that the project is finished with a technique called "crayon resist," in which a watercolor wash is brushed over a picture colored with crayons. The wax of the crayons resists, or pushes away, the watercolors and creates an interesting effect.

Tell children that they will create a picture of overlapping apples using the crayon resist technique. Pass out the materials and demonstrate the procedures as children follow along.

Timesaving Tip!

Set up your watercolor paint station ahead of time. Cover a table with newspaper and place the watercolors, water containers, and paintbrushes on it. You might cover all the colors in the paint tray except blue and purple with masking tape.

Step by Step

1. Using a pencil, draw three or more overlapping apples on the white paper. You might refer to the apple display for inspiration. You can draw the entire shape for each apple and then erase the lines on the parts of the apples that are to be hidden by other apples.

Erase overlapping lines.

2. When the overlapping apples look the way you want them, trace the lines with a black crayon, pressing firmly to make heavy lines.

3. Color each apple red, green, or yellow. You can color all the apples the same color or use a combination of colors. While coloring, press firmly and be sure to fill in each apple as completely as possible. If you included stems and leaves on the apples, color these as well.

4. Take the project to the watercolor paint station. Spread a wash of blue or purple watercolor paint over the picture. As you paint, notice how the crayon pushes away the paint and makes the colored apples look brighter.

One Step More

Display the projects around the border of a bulletin board featuring apples. Or use them as a centerpiece for the bulletin board display.

Language Arts Link

Have children brainstorm a list of words that can be used to describe apples, such as *red, smooth, crunchy,* and *sweet.* (Encourage them to draw from their sensory explorations with apples.) When finished, explain that words used to describe an object are called adjectives. Then, have children write sentences about apples using some of the adjectives on the list. More advanced children can use the adjectives in a story or rhyme about apples.

Related Reading

Apples by Gail Gibbons (Holiday House, 2000)

How Do Apples Grow? by Betsy Maestro (HarperTrophy, 1993)

I Am an Apple by Jean Marzollo (Scholastic, 1997)

The Seasons of Arnold's Apple Tree by Gail Gibbons (Voyager, 1988)

Warm 'n' Cool Landscapes

Use these projects to encourage children to explore and compare the warm and cool temperatures related to autumn days.

Art Concepts

warm colors
cool colors
landscape

Materials

To display:
- color wheel (page 197)
- completed project

For each child:
- 9- by 12-inch white construction paper
- pencil
- fine-tip black permanent marker

To share:
- red, yellow, orange, blue, green, and purple oil pastels (one of each color for every two children)

Let's Begin

Point out the red, yellow, and orange sections of the color wheel. Tell children that these are called warm colors because they suggest warmth. Point to blue, green, and purple. What do children think these colors are called? Explain that these are cool colors because they suggest coolness. Next, show children the completed project. Tell them that one side of the landscape—or picture of the land— is colored in warm colors and the other side is in cool colors. Continue by telling children that the warm side represents an early fall day, when the weather is still fairly warm, while the cool side represents a cooler day in late fall. Point out details on each side that show signs of either early or late fall.

Tell children that they will create a fall landscape featuring warm and cool colors. Pass out the materials and demonstrate the procedures as children follow along.

Timesaving Tip!

To help avoid smearing the colored areas of the page and eliminate hand-washing trips to the sink, have children color their pictures from left to right and top to bottom.

Step by Step

1. Fold the white paper in half and then unfold it. Use a pencil to draw a simple landscape on the entire page. You might draw a city, small neighborhood, mountains, river scene, and so on.

2. Working on the left side of the fold in your paper, add details to represent a warmer day in early fall, such as leaves on the trees, people in long–sleeve shirts, and seasonal fruit (apples, pumpkins, and so on). On the right side, add things that might be seen on a cooler day in late fall, such as trees with bare branches, people in jackets, and fading grass.

Warm Side — Yellow, Orange, Red

Cool Side — Blue, Green, Purple

3. Trace the pencil drawing with the black marker.

4. Use oil pastels in warm colors (red, yellow, and orange) to color the left side of the picture. Then, use oil pastels in cool colors (blue, green, and purple) to color the right side.

One Step More

Display the projects one above another on a wall. Each day during fall, post the day's temperature next to one of the projects, starting at the top left and moving down the display. When you reach the bottom, return to the top and work down the right side. Have children use the display to compare the temperatures of early and late fall.

Language Arts Link

List on chart paper several homonyms (words with double meanings), such as *bat, fall, leaves, park, present,* and *shop.* Explain to children that while their landscapes represent the same scene on both sides of the paper, the warm and cool colors give each side of the scene a different meaning. Similarly, the listed words are always spelled the same, but each one has two or more meanings. To demonstrate, use the same word in two sentences, but use a different meaning for the word in each sentence. Then, invite children to choose three homonyms, write a sentence with each one, and illustrate the sentence to show what it means. More advanced children can create a homonym dictionary to use in their writing activities.

Related Reading

How Do You Know It's Fall? by Allan Fowler (Children's Press, 1992)

It's Fall by Linda Glaser (Millbrook Press, 2001)

When Autumn Falls by Kelly Nidey (Albert Whitman & Company, 2004)

Sponge-Print Fall Trees

To reinforce the color-changing process of leaves, invite children to create these beautiful fall trees.

Art Concepts

warm colors
texture
sponge print

Let's Begin

Show children the pictures of fall trees. Explain that during autumn in many areas, the leaves change color and fall off the trees. Do children see red, yellow, and orange leaves on the pictured trees? Explain that these colors are called warm colors because they suggest warmth. Then, have children examine the tree and leaves on the completed project. Tell them that the darker lines on the trunk give the appearance of bark. The uneven coloring of the sponge prints make the tree look like it's filled with colorful leaves. Techniques that create an appearance of texture, like the bark and leaves, help make a picture look more realistic.

Inform children that they will create a fall tree using warm colors and texture to help make it look more real. Pass out the materials and demonstrate the procedures as children follow along.

Materials

To display:
- pictures of trees with colorful leaves
- completed project

For each child:
- 12- by 18-inch manila construction paper
- pencil

To share:
- oil pastels (one box for every two children)

For sponge-printing stations:
- twelve 1-inch square sponges
- shallow trays of red, yellow, and orange tempera paint

Timesaving Tip!

Set up three sponge-printing stations ahead of time. Cover each table with newspaper and place a paint tray and four sponges on it. Add a half-inch layer of moist paper towels to each paint tray. Just before beginning the activity, spread a different color paint onto the towels in each tray.

Step by Step

1. Place the manila paper in a vertical (tall) position on the table. Using a pencil, draw a small dot about four fingers distance from the bottom of the page. Then, draw a tree trunk from this point upward. About halfway up the page, draw branches that extend from the trunk to the sides and top of the paper. Add smaller branches as well.

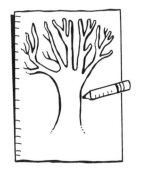

2. Draw a zigzag line across the bottom of the tree to represent the base of the trunk. Then, pencil in other objects of interest, such as a bird in the tree, a squirrel near the trunk, or a swing hanging from a branch.

3. Working from the top of the page to the bottom (to prevent smearing), trace and color the trunk and tree branches with a light brown oil pastel. Next, color the other objects in the picture. You might also add grass across the bottom of the page.

4. To make leaves, take the tree to the red, yellow, and orange sponge-printing stations. Use the sponges and paint to print "leaves" on the branches of the tree, falling from the tree, and in piles on the ground. Press the sponges lightly onto the picture, overlapping colors to achieve a colorful, realistic effect, but avoid covering the branches and other objects completely with prints.

One Step More

Display the projects on a wall or bulletin board, staggering and overlapping them to give the appearance of the woods. Invite children to border the fantastic fall display with their fall-inspired creative writings.

Language Arts Link

Tell children that *tree* begins with the blend *tr*. Ask them to brainstorm other words that begin with *tr*, such as *trail, trip, train, trouble,* and *trap*. List their responses on chart paper. Then, have children use words from the list to make up a class story. Instruct them to take turns adding to the story so that every child has a chance to contribute. Later, you might challenge more advanced children to write the words from the list in alphabetical order.

Related Reading

Autumn Leaves by Ken Robbins (Scholastic Press, 1998)

Fall, Leaves, Fall! by Zoe Hall (Scholastic Press, 2000)

Why Do Leaves Change Color? by Betsy Maestro (HarperTrophy, 1994)

Radial Leaf Rounds

*After children learn about the parts of a leaf, have them create
these symmetrical designs to reinforce their leaf-related vocabulary.*

Art Concepts
shape
symmetry
radial

Materials

To display:
- leaves in different shapes, sizes, and colors
- completed project

For each child:
- 9-inch white construction paper circle
- pencil
- fine-tip black permanent marker
- crayons

To share:
- 10 tagboard templates for each leaf shape (page 172)

Let's Begin

Display the leaves and identify each part of a leaf: the blade, stem, and veins. Point out the center vein in a leaf. Is the shape of the leaf the same on both sides of the vein? Explain that when an object's shape is the same on both sides of a centerline, the object is symmetrical. Then, show children the completed project and ask if they see symmetry in it. Help them understand that each leaf has symmetry, but also that the leaf in each section is symmetrical to the leaves in the other sections. Continue by explaining to them that just as the spokes of a bicycle wheel extend—or radiate—from a central point, the leaf designs on the project radiate from the center of the circle. This kind of symmetry is called radial symmetry.

Tell children that they will use leaf designs to create a project with radial symmetry. Pass out the materials and demonstrate the procedures as children follow along.

Timesaving Tip!

You might provide 9-inch paper plates instead of the paper circles. After creating the fold lines, children can flatten their plates to trace and color the leaves in the four sections.

Step by Step

1. Fold the white circle in half. Then, fold it in half again. Unfold the circle to reveal four sections created by the fold lines.

2. Choose a leaf template. Position the leaf on one section of the circle so that it fits completely into the section. Use a pencil to trace the outline of the leaf. In the same manner, trace the leaf template onto each of the other sections of the circle. Be sure to place the leaf in the same position on each section.

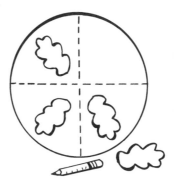

3. Add a stem and veins to each leaf, trying to make all the leaves as identical as possible. Then, trace all the leaves with the black marker.

4. Use one autumn-related color to color all the leaves on your circle.

5. Choose another autumn color to color the area around the leaf in each section. You can use the same or a different color for the background in each section.

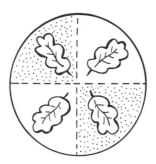

One Step More

Display the projects on an autumn-related bulletin board. Have children add labels to point out the different parts of their leaves (*blade*, *veins*, and *stem*).

Language Arts Link

Write *leaf* and *leaves* on the chalkboard. Tell children that *leaf* is the singular form of the noun while *leaves* is the plural form. Explain that to make plurals from most singular nouns ending in *f* or *fe*, the *f* is changed to *v* and *s* or *es* is added to the word. List other nouns that end in *f* or *fe*, such as *calf*, *dwarf*, *half*, *hoof*, *knife*, *life*, *scarf*, *self*, *shelf*, *thief*, *wife*, and *wolf*. Then, have volunteers write the plural form of the words. Afterward, ask children to illustrate both the singular and plural forms of three words from the list. More advanced children might use the words in sentences to describe their drawings.

Related Reading

Leaf Man by Lois Ehlert (Harcourt Children's Books, 2005)

Look What I Did With a Leaf! by Morteza E. Sohi (Walker Books for Young Readers, 1995)

Red Leaf, Yellow Leaf by Lois Ehlert (Harcourt Children's Books, 1991)

Patchwork Pumpkin Weave

*Create these unique woven pumpkins to introduce or wrap up
a sensory study on this favorite fall fruit.*

Art Concepts
shape
line
pattern

Materials

To display:
- pumpkin
- completed project

For each child:
- 9- by 12-inch orange construction paper
- pencil
- scissors
- six 1½- by 8-inch strips of white construction paper
- crayons

To share:
- 12 tagboard pumpkin templates (page 173)
- glue sticks
- scraps of green paper

Let's Begin

Invite children to examine the pumpkin and talk about its shape. Point out its curved, rounded features and the vertical ridges on its surface. Then, show them the completed project. Do children see vertical lines on the project? What other kinds of lines do they see? Be sure to point out the horizontal cut lines. Next, draw their attention to the colorful sections. Explain that each of these sections is part of a strip of paper that has been decorated with a pattern and then woven into the pumpkin shape. The woven strips give the pumpkin a patchwork appearance. Finally, ask children to identify patterns on the project.

Tell children that they will create a woven patchwork pumpkin with patterned strips of paper. Pass out the materials and demonstrate the procedures as children follow along.

Timesaving Tip!
You might pre-cut the pumpkin shapes and then have children start at Step 2 to make their projects.

Step by Step

1. Fold the orange paper in half. Place the straight edge of the pumpkin pattern on the fold, fitting it to the paper. Use a pencil to trace the shape. Cut along the pencil outline through both layers of the folded paper.

2. Keeping the cutout folded, lightly pencil in a vertical line about one inch from the curved side of the shape. Then, draw four horizontal lines from the fold to the vertical line. You can use straight, curvy, or zigzag lines. Draw the top and bottom lines at least one inch away from the edges of the cutout.

3. Cut along each horizontal line, starting at the fold and stopping at the vertical line. Be sure to cut through both layers of the folded shape. Open the shape to reveal a pumpkin with four horizontal cuts in it.

4. Use crayons to draw a different pattern on each white paper strip. You might combine two or three lines, shapes, or colors to create each pattern.

5. Weave the paper strips in an over-and-under motion through the horizontal cuts in the pumpkin cutout. Alternate the weaving pattern for each strip. Slide the strips close together so that they all fit.

6. Trim the ends of each paper strip to fit the cutout and then glue the ends in place. Cut out a stem from green paper. Glue the stem to the patchwork pumpkin.

One Step More

Twist a long strip of green bulletin board paper to create a pumpkin vine. Attach the pumpkins to the vine. Display the pumpkin vine around a seasonal bulletin board.

Language Arts Link

Say the words *patchwork* and *pumpkin*. Ask children to tell how the two words are similar. Guide them to understand that both begin with *p* and have two syllables. Then, invite them to name other *p* words that contain two syllables, such as *pickle*, *piglet*, *police*, *popcorn*, and *purple*. Afterward, have them pair up two-syllable *p* words to create real or silly phrases to illustrate (such as a *purple pickle*). More advanced children might make up alliterative rhymes with their phrases.

Related Reading

Pumpkin Circle: The Story of a Garden by George Levenson (Tricycle Press, 2002)

The Pumpkin Book by Gail Gibbons (Holiday House, 2000)

The Pumpkin Patch by Elizabeth King (Puffin, 1996)

Pumpkin Pumpkin by Jeanne Titherington (Greenwillow, 1986)

Lifelike Watercolor Scarecrows

Farmers have important jobs, but so do scarecrows! Invite children to create these mixed-media scarecrows to celebrate farm workers.

Art Concepts
line
shape
texture

Materials

To display:
- pictures of scarecrows (see Related Reading for books featuring scarecrow pictures)
- completed project

For each child:
- 12- by 18-inch white construction paper
- pencil
- black permanent marker

To share:
- assorted craft items including wiggle eyes, raffia, yarn, scraps of fabric and burlap, and buttons
- glue sticks

For watercolor paint station:
- watercolor paints
- paintbrushes
- containers of water

Let's Begin

Invite children to examine the scarecrow pictures. Discuss the appearance of the scarecrows. How do they resemble people? What are they made of? How are they dressed? Then, show children the completed project. Point out the different kinds of lines and shapes used in the project. Draw children's attention to the parts of the project in which fabric, buttons, and other craft items are used. Explain that these items give the scarecrow texture and help make it look more lifelike (or realistic).

Tell children that they will make a lifelike scarecrow using watercolors and a variety of craft items. Pass out the materials and demonstrate the procedures as children follow along.

Timesaving Tip!

Set up a watercolor paint station ahead of time. Cover a table with newspaper and place the watercolors, water containers, and paintbrushes on it.

Step by Step

1. Fold the white paper into thirds, lightly creasing the folds. Then, unfold the paper. Using a pencil, draw a circle about the size of a cookie just above the top fold line. This will be your scarecrow's head. Do not add any other details at this time.

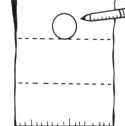

2. Draw the scarecrow's shirt in the middle section of your paper. You can use an oval or rectangle for the shirt. Be sure to draw the shape from the top to the bottom fold lines to make the body proportionate to the head. To make the scarecrow look like it's propped up on a post, you might draw the arms outward along the top fold line and then bent down at the elbows. Keep your drawing simple and free of details for now.

3. Draw the scarecrow's pants on the bottom section of the paper. You can use two tall rectangles to represent the pant legs. When finished, trace the entire scarecrow with the black marker.

4. Take the scarecrow to the watercolor paint station. Paint each part of the scarecrow with the paint color of your choice. Then, set the painting aside to dry.

5. Use craft items to add details to the scarecrow. You might glue on a yarn mouth, felt nose, and wiggle eyes, as well as a burlap hat and raffia hair, hands, and feet. You might also add fabric patches and buttons to the scarecrow's clothes.

One Step More

Create a cornfield display on a bulletin board. Have children cut loosely around the outline of their scarecrows. Then, display the scarecrows as the feature attraction in the cornfield.

Language Arts Link

Tell children that *lifelike*, *watercolor*, and *scarecrow* are examples of compound words. Explain that when two words are put together to make one word, a compound word is formed. Have children generate a list of other compound words. Then, ask them to choose five compound words and write each of the two words that make up each compound word on a separate index card. Encourage small groups to use their word cards to create as many new compound words as possible. Have them list and then share their words with another group. Challenge more advanced children to write their group's words in alphabetical order.

Related Reading

Jeb Scarecrow's Pumpkin Patch by Jana Dillon (Houghton Mifflin, 1995)

Little Scarecrow Boy by Margaret Wise Brown (Joanna Cotler, 1998)

Scarecrow by Cynthia Rylant (Voyager Books, 2001)

The Scarecrow's Hat by Ken Brown (Peachtree Publishers, 2001)

Torn-Paper Owl

Invite children to use these fine-feathered friends to share their owl knowledge with others.

Art Concepts
shape
warm colors
torn paper

Let's Begin

Invite children to examine the owl pictures and describe some of the shapes they see on the birds. Point out the round faces, triangle-shaped beaks, and pointy talons. Tell children that many owls have oval-shaped bodies. Then, display the completed project. In what ways does the project resemble a real owl? Draw children's attention to the colors used on the project. Explain that warm colors (red, yellow, and orange) of torn paper have been used to create the owl and its feathery texture.

Tell children that they will use warm colors to make a torn-paper owl. Pass out the materials and demonstrate the procedures as children follow along.

Materials

To display:
- pictures of owls (see Related Reading for books featuring owl pictures)
- completed project

For each child:
- two 1½-inch squares of black construction paper (for eyes)
- pencil

To share:
- 9- by 12-inch red, yellow, and orange construction paper
- glue sticks

Timesaving Tip!

Rather than drawing the half-oval and half-circle on their folded papers, you might have children tear these shapes freehanded. Remind them that they can use torn-paper feathers to cover up any irregular tears.

Step by Step

1. Choose red, yellow, or orange paper for the owl's body. Fold the paper in half lengthwise. Use a pencil to draw a half-oval on the paper, starting and ending at the fold. Draw the shape as large as possible. Slowly tear along the lines through both layers of the folded paper. Unfold the paper to reveal a large oval.

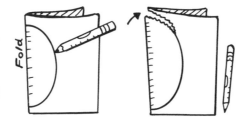

2. Choose a color for the head. Fold the paper in half crosswise, draw a half-circle on it (starting and ending at the fold), and tear along the lines through both layers. Unfold the paper to reveal a circle.

3. Choose a color for the wings. Fold the paper in half lengthwise. Draw as large an oval as possible on the paper. Tear out the oval through both layers.

4. Place the owl's head and wings on the body. If you want to make any of the pieces smaller, simply tear them to the size you want. Then, glue the parts of the owl together.

5. Tear off the corners of each black square to make round eyes. Glue the eyes onto your owl.

6. Use your leftover scraps of paper to tear a beak, ear tufts, talons, and feathers to glue onto the owl.

One Step More

Roll several lengths of brown bulletin board paper to use as a tree trunk and branches. Crush the rolled paper and then assemble the pieces on a wall to create a tree. Attach the torn-paper owls to the branches.

Language Arts Link

Ask children to name words that contain the same vowel sound as *owl*. Write their responses on chart paper. Then, review the words, looking closely at the spelling of each one. Most likely, words spelled with *ow* and *ou* will appear on the list. Tell children that this vowel sound can be represented by both spellings. Later, write on index cards words from the list that children need to know. Pair up children and have them use the cards as flash cards to practice reading the words. You might have more advanced children practice spelling the words.

Related Reading

All About Owls by Jim Arnosky (Scholastic Press, 1995)

Owl Moon by Jane Yolen (Philomel, 1987)

See How They Grow: Owl by Mary Ling (Dorling Kindersley, 1992)

Welcome to the World of Owls by Diane Swanson (Walrus Books, 1997)

3-D Spiders

Display these special spiders in your room to help reinforce children's spider knowledge.

Art Concepts

color
line
shape
pattern
three-dimensional

Materials

To display:
- pictures of spiders (see Related Reading for books featuring spider pictures)
- completed project

For each child:
- 4- by 9-inch black construction paper
- 3- by 9-inch black construction paper
- eight 1- by 9-inch strips of black construction paper

To share:
- oil pastels
- glue sticks
- stapler

Let's Begin

Use the spider pictures to point out and review different features of these creatures, such as their many eyes, eight legs, fangs, and draglines. Then, show children the completed project. Ask them to name the colors found on the spider. What kinds of lines and shapes are used on it? Do they see any patterns? Point out that different sizes of paper have been used to construct the spider. Finally, explain that the spider project differs from the spider pictures because it has three dimensions—height, width, and depth.

Tell children that they will create a 3-D spider decorated with patterns on its body and legs. Pass out the materials and demonstrate the procedures as children follow along.

Timesaving Tip!

Use a paper cutter to cut the black construction paper into the sizes needed for the project. You can stack and cut several sheets at a time.

Step by Step

1. Use the 4- by 9-inch black paper for the spider's body. Place the paper in a vertical (tall) position on the table. Use oil pastels to draw a pattern on the paper. You might use a combination of lines, shapes, and colors. Be sure to draw the pattern on the entire length of the paper. When finished, glue the ends of the paper together to create a loop.

2. For the head, place the 3- by 9-inch black paper in a vertical position on the table. Draw eyes and fangs in the middle of the paper. (Remind children that all spiders have fangs and most have eight eyes!) Draw a pattern above and below the spider's face. Then, glue the ends together to form a loop.

3. Staple the head to the spider's body.

4. For the spider's eight legs, draw a pattern on each of the 1- by 9-inch strips of black paper. Accordion-fold each leg. Then glue the legs to the spider's body.

One Step More

Add a dragline to the spider. Punch two holes in the spider's body and attach a 12-inch length of string to it. To display, suspend the spiders from windows, doorways, and learning centers.

Language Arts Link

Help your class generate a list of words that begin with *sp* (as in *spider*). After reviewing the words, ask children to form a circle. Then, pass a toy spider around circle while playing music. Periodically stop the music and tell the child holding the spider, "Spider speak!" That child will then use a word that begins with *sp* in a sentence. You can use "Spider spell!" with more advanced children, and then call out a word that begins with *sp* for them to spell.

Related Reading

Amazing Spiders by Dorling Kindersley Ltd (Knopf Books for Young Readers; 1990)

Diary of a Spider by Doreen Cronin (Joanna Cotler, 2005)

Dream Weaver by Jonathan London (Silver Whistle, 1998)

Spiders by Gail Gibbons (Holiday House, 1994)

Miniature *Mayflower* in a Bottle

Use these miniature ships to review the Mayflower's historical voyage to a new land.

Art Concepts
shape
texture
overlap

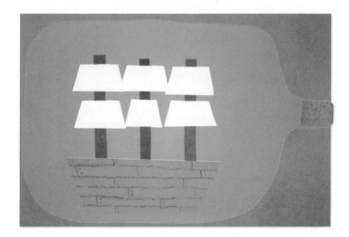

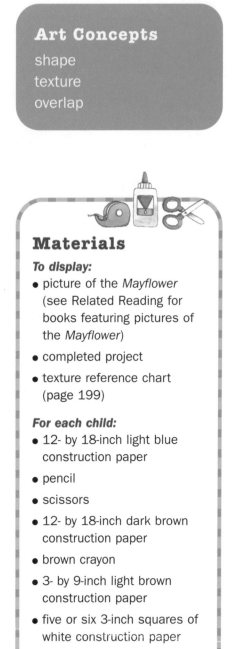

Materials

To display:
- picture of the *Mayflower* (see Related Reading for books featuring pictures of the *Mayflower*)
- completed project
- texture reference chart (page 199)

For each child:
- 12- by 18-inch light blue construction paper
- pencil
- scissors
- 12- by 18-inch dark brown construction paper
- brown crayon
- 3- by 9-inch light brown construction paper
- five or six 3-inch squares of white construction paper
- 2- by 6-inch black construction paper

To share:
- glue sticks

Let's Begin

Show children a picture of the *Mayflower*. Remind them that this is the ship that brought the Pilgrims to America in 1620. Point out the wooden hull, sails, and masts. Then, show children the completed project. What shapes do they see? Help them identify trapezoids, and triangles, rectangles and squares, if you have used them in your completed project sample. Have them examine the ship's hull. Explain that the lines drawn across the hull give the appearance of wood. Ask children to refer to the texture reference chart to find other designs that might resemble the appearance, or texture, of wood. Finally, note that some of the sails partially cover other sails. Explain that overlapping is another technique that artists use to make their work look more realistic.

Tell children that they will use texture and overlapping to create their own version of a *Mayflower* in a bottle. Pass out the materials and demonstrate the procedures as children follow along.

TimeSaving Tip!
Use a paper cutter to cut the light brown, white, and black construction paper into the sizes needed for the project. You can stack and cut several sheets at a time.

Step by Step

1. Use the pencil to draw a large bottle shape on the light blue paper. Cut out the shape and glue it onto the dark brown paper.

2. To make the ship's hull, draw a diagonal line from each top corner of the 3- by 9-inch brown paper to about one inch from the bottom corner. Cut along the lines. Use the brown crayon to draw lines across the resulting trapezoid to create the appearance of a wooden hull. Then, position the bottle so that it looks like its lying on its side. Glue the hull onto the bottle near the bottom of the page.

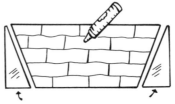

3. Cut out six sails from the white squares. You might make a trapezoidal sail by cutting diagonally from each top corner of the square to about ½ inch from the bottom corner. Or you might cut a square in half diagonally to create two triangular sails, or cut ½ inch off of one side of a square for a rectangular sail. You might also decide to use the white square as a sail.

Some ways to cut sails.

4. Cut the black paper into three strips to create masts for the ship. Position the masts and sails onto the ship so that they all fit on the bottle shape. (Be sure to overlap some of the sails.) Once you have the shapes where you want them, glue the pieces down.

One Step More

To make a bottle cork, cut a rectangle from the leftover brown paper. Dot the cork with the brown crayon to create texture. Then, glue it onto the mouth end of the bottle.

Language Arts Link

Encourage children to imagine they were pilgrims on the *Mayflower*. What kind of things might they experience? Invite them to create a three- or four-panel cartoon strip to illustrate some of their experiences. Have them write or dictate a caption for each panel. Ask more advanced children to create a longer cartoon strip that illustrates a series of events in their imaginary journey.

Related Reading

...*If You Sailed on the Mayflower in 1620* by Ann McGovern (Scholastic, 1991)

Mayflower 1620: A New Look at a Pilgrim Village by Catherine O'Neill Grace, Peter Arenstam, and John Kemp with Plimoth Plantation (National Geographic Children's Books 1, 2003)

On the Mayflower: Voyage of the Ship's Apprentice & a Passenger Girl by Kate Waters (Scholastic Press, 1996)

Mixed-Media Thanksgiving Basket

Celebrate the nutritious foods of the harvest with this Thanksgiving basket filled with textured produce.

Art Concepts

line
shape
texture
overlap

Materials

To display:
- basket of fruit or vegetables
- completed project
- texture reference chart (page 199)

For each child:
- 9- by 12-inch light brown construction paper
- scissors
- pencil
- black crayon

To share:
- scraps of different types and colors of paper (wallpaper, foil and embossed wrapping paper, tissue paper, crepe paper, corrugated paper, and so on)
- scraps of different types and textures of fabric (felt, burlap, corduroy, netting, and so on)
- glue

Let's Begin

Remind children that the Pilgrims celebrated a plentiful harvest during the first Thanksgiving. Show them the produce-filled basket and the completed project. Have them describe and compare the shapes, designs, and textures they see. Explain that the basket weave lines on the project give the appearance of texture and help make the basket look more real. Ask children to refer to the texture reference chart to find other designs that might resemble the texture of a basket. Then, call their attention to how the overlapping foods also create a more realistic appearance. Finally, tell children that this is a mixed-media project because it was created with two or more kinds of art materials. Have them identify some of the materials used in the project.

Tell children that they will use texture and overlapping to create a Thanksgiving basket of fruits and vegetables. Pass out the materials and demonstrate the procedures as children follow along.

Timesaving Tip!

To help children create proportionately sized foods, precut 3- to 5-inch squares of the scrap paper and fabrics (use a paper cutter to cut the paper). Have children draw their foods onto the squares and cut them out.

Step by Step

1. To make a basket, fold the brown paper in half. Cut through both layers of paper to round off one corner opposite the fold. Unfold the paper to reveal a bowl-shaped basket.

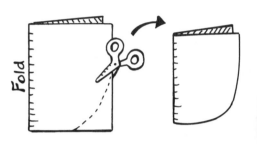

2. Use a pencil to draw a basket weave pattern on the cutout. You can refer to the texture reference chart for ideas, then trace the pattern with a black crayon.

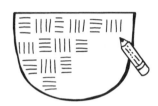

3. Choose several different materials to use for the foods you want to put in the basket. Use a pencil to draw the shape onto the material and then cut out the shape. You might cut out burlap potatoes, crepe paper ears of corn, gold foil squash, and so on.

4. Position the foods along the top of the basket (be sure to overlap some of the shapes). Once you have the shapes where you want them, glue the pieces onto the basket.

Glue food.

One Step More

To create a contrasting background, mount the project on a 12- by 18-inch sheet of white construction paper.

Language Arts Link

Before making the project, share with children Lois Ehlert's *Eating the Alphabet: Fruits & Vegetables From A to Z* (Voyager Books, 1993). Then, encourage them to include foods in their baskets that all begin with different letters. More advanced children might write a mystery word on the back of their basket and then feature a different food in the basket to represent each letter in the word. They can challenge classmates to use the food clues to try to guess the mystery word.

Related Reading

Alligator Arrived With Apples: A Potluck Alphabet Feast by Crescent Dragonwagon (Aladdin, 1992)

Growing Vegetable Soup by Lois Ehlert (Voyager Books, 1990)

The Surprise Garden by Zoe Hall (Scholastic, 1998)

3-D Textured Turkeys

These stand-up turkeys can be used as a Thanksgiving table centerpiece and a conversation starter for children to share their turkey knowledge.

Art Concepts

pattern
texture
three-dimensional

Materials

To display:
- pictures of turkeys (see Related Reading for books featuring turkey pictures)
- completed project

For each child:
- 12- by 18-inch light brown construction paper
- pencil
- scissors
- 5- by 10-inch orange tissue paper
- 2 wiggle eyes

To share:
- 12 tagboard turkey templates (page 174)
- glue sticks
- stapler
- scraps of red tissue paper

For sponge-printing stations:
- twelve 1-inch square sponges
- shallow trays of yellow, orange, and brown tempera paint

Let's Begin

Use the turkey pictures to point out and review different features of these birds, such as the unusual skin growths known as snoods, wattles, caruncles, and the fan of tail feathers. Then, show children the completed project. Call their attention to how the feathers on the turkey's body appear to have a soft-looking appearance. Explain that this texture was created by lightly sponge-printing a pattern of colored squares onto the body. Point out that the tissue paper features around the head and the fan-like tail feathers make the turkey look more realistic. Finally, tell them that the project differs from the turkey pictures because it has three dimensions—height, width, and depth.

Inform children that they will create a stand-up 3-D turkey. Then, pass out the materials and demonstrate the procedures as children follow along.

Timesaving Tip!

Set up three sponge-printing stations ahead of time. Cover each table with newspaper, place a paint tray and four sponges on it, and add a half-inch layer of moist paper towels to each paint tray. Just before beginning the activity, spread a different color paint onto the towels in each tray.

Step by Step

1. Fold the brown paper in half. Place the turkey template on the paper with the head along the fold. Trace the shape with a pencil and then cut it out through both layers of the folded paper, being sure not to cut through the fold.

2. Unfold the cutout and take it to the sponge-printing stations. To make feathers, use the sponges and paint to print a pattern of colored squares onto the cutout. Press the sponges lightly onto the cutout, overlapping the prints to achieve a soft, feathery effect.

3. After the paint dries, fold the straight edges of the cutout and glue them together to create a base for the turkey, as shown.

4. For the tail, fan-fold the orange tissue paper and staple one end between the tail ends of the turkey. Spread out the top of the fan.

5. Twist a short piece of red tissue paper to create a snood. Then, wrinkle up a small scrap of red tissue paper to make the wattle. Glue the snood and wattle between the two sides of the turkey, as shown. Drape the snood over the beak.

6. Add a wiggle eye to each side of the turkey's head.

One Step More

Cover the turkey's beak with yellow tissue paper or construction paper.

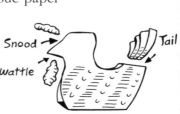

Fold, overlap, and glue.

Snood → Wattle → Tail

Language Arts Link

Explain that the vowel in *turkey* is an *r*-controlled vowel. Have children brainstorm other words that contain the same *r*-controlled vowel sound as in *turkey*, such as *her, bird, shirt, word,* and *burn*. Then, display a large turkey on a bulletin board. Each time children come across a word with a similar *r*-controlled vowel in their reading materials, have them write the word on an index card and attach it to the display. Periodically review the words with your class. You might have more advanced children write Thanksgiving-related sentences with the words they find.

Related Reading

Gracias, the Thanksgiving Turkey by Joy Cowley (Scholastic, 1996)

A Plump and Perky Turkey by Teresa Bateman (Marshall Cavendish Corporation, 2004)

A Thanksgiving Turkey by Julian Scheer (Holiday House, 2001)

A Turkey for Thanksgiving by Eve Bunting (Clarion Books, 1995)

In the Style of M. C. Escher: Colorful Tessellation Creations

These M. C. Escher-inspired tessellation creations can be used to explore shapes, patterns, symmetry, sorting, counting, and more!

Materials

To display:

- *Symmetry E118* by M. C. Escher (page 201)
- samples of wallpaper and fabric that contain tessellations (optional)
- completed project

For each child:

- 4-inch square of plain white index card
- pencil
- scissors
- tape
- 12- by 18-inch white construction paper

To share:

- crayons

Let's Begin

Tell children that the Dutch artist M. C. Escher is famous for creating fascinating tessellation designs. Explain that a tessellation is a pattern made up of designs that fit together and repeat over and over. Then, have children examine the Escher print to identify the shapes and repeating patterns used in its creation. Point out how the artist connects the different colored lizards to create an interesting and colorful pattern. Tell them that the patterns of lizards in the print are symmetrical. That is, each colored lizard touches an identical but flipped version of itself. Can children find the patterns of symmetry in the print? Afterward, show them the completed project and any wallpaper and fabric samples that feature tessellations. Have them identify the designs, patterns, and symmetry on the project and samples.

Tell children that they will design and make their own colorful tessellation creations. Pass out the materials and demonstrate the procedures as children follow along.

Timesaving Tip!

In advance, make a variety of templates from the 4-inch square cards. Invite children to choose one of the pre-made templates and start at Step 2 to make their project.

Step by Step

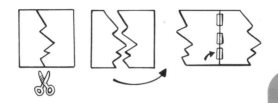

1. To make a tessellation template, draw a curvy, zigzag, or other kind of interesting line from the top of the 4-inch square card to the bottom. Cut along the line to cut the card into two pieces. Then, tape the two long straight edges of the card together.

2. Use a pencil to trace the template onto the top left corner of the white paper. Then, slide the template to the right so that the left edge fits along the outline of the penciled-in shape. Trace the template again (you don't need to redraw the shared lines between the two shapes). Continue sliding and tracing the template until you reach the right edge of the paper.

3. Place the template under the top left outline. Trace the template and then slide and trace it again, as in Step 2. Repeat, drawing rows of tessellations until the page is filled.

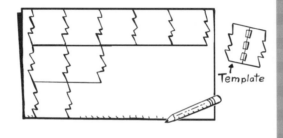

Template

4. Color the tessellations with two or three different colors, creating a color pattern as you go along. Be sure to color any space along the edges of the paper that make up only part of a tessellation. When finished, you might add identical details to all the shapes to make them look like faces, critters, and so on.

One Step More

Display the projects with the Escher print, using the title "Tessellation Inspirations."

Language Arts Link

Tell children that just as tessellations are made up of repeating patterns so is a word family made up of repeated spelling patterns in words. Write a few words that belong to different word families on the board. Invite children to add words to each family and identify the repeated spelling pattern in the words. Then, have them create two-line rhymes using words from the same word family. Ask more advanced children to use words from a selected word family to make up longer rhymes or create songs to the tune of common childhood songs.

Related Reading

All About Lizards by Jim Arnosky (Scholastic, 2004)

An Optical Artist: Exploring Patterns and Symmetry by Greg Roza (PowerKids Press, 2005)

Leaping Lizards by Stuart J. Murphy (HarperTrophy, 2005)

Let's Fly a Kite by Stuart J. Murphy (HarperTrophy, 2000)

Cardboard-Print Menorah

Invite children to use these special menorahs to share about the origins and traditions of the eight-day Hanukkah celebration.

Art Concepts

pattern
color
printmaking

Materials

To display:
- several pictures of menorahs (from catalogs or books in Related Reading that feature menorahs)
- completed project

For each child:
- 12- by 18-inch blue construction paper
- pencil
- glue stick

To share:
- scraps of different kinds of paper in blue, white, yellow, gold, silver, or any combination of these colors (construction paper, stationery, wrapping paper, and so on)

For printmaking stations:
- twenty 1- by 4-inch strips of corrugated cardboard
- several shallow trays of white and light blue tempera paint

Let's Begin

Display the menorah pictures and ask children to share what they know about menorahs. Afterward, explain that a menorah is the candle-holder used during Hanukkah. The shamash—the center candle—always has the highest position in the menorah and is used to light the other eight candles. Do the candles make a pattern? Point out the four candles on each side of the shamash. Then, show children the completed project. Ask them to identify the material used to make the menorah (torn paper). What colors are the candles? Tell them that blue and white are the colors of the Israeli flag. Finally, explain that the candles in the menorah are made from cardboard prints.

Let children know that they will create a torn-paper menorah with cardboard-print candles. Pass out the materials and demonstrate the procedures as children follow along.

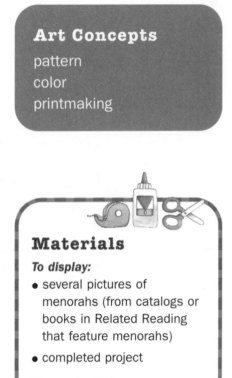

Timesaving Tip!

Set up two printmaking stations ahead of time. Cover each table with newspaper and place several paint trays and ten cardboard strips on it. Add a half-inch layer of moist paper towels to each paint tray. Just before beginning the activity, spread the white and blue paints onto the towels in the trays.

Step by Step

1. Place the blue construction paper in a horizontal position on the table. Use a pencil to draw a line across the paper about one hand-width above the bottom edge. This bottom section represents the menorah.

2. To decorate the menorah, tear scraps of paper into small pieces and glue them in the section at the bottom of the paper. Glue a few extra pieces of torn paper at the top center of the menorah, where the shamash will be placed.

3. Take the project to the printmaking stations. Use a cardboard strip to print a candle—the shamash—on the tall center part of the menorah. Then, print four candles onto the menorah on each side of the shamash. You might use the same color paint for each candle or alternate the colors to create a color pattern.

↑ Torn paper

Cardboard Strip

White paint

One Step More

After the candle prints dry, cut out and glue a yellow or red tissue-paper flame to the top of each candle.

Language Arts Link

The glow from the candles in a menorah represents light. Invite children to list words on chart paper that belong to the word families for *light* and *glow* (such as *might, night, right, sight, tight* and *blow, grow, know, row, throw*). Then, have them use words from the list to create simple rhymes about Hanukkah. More advanced children might use the words to write longer rhymes or short stories related to the eight-day celebration.

Related Reading

Eight Days of Hanukkah by Harriet Ziefert (Viking, 1997)

Hanukkah: A Counting Book in English, Hebrew, and Yiddish by Emily Sper (Scholastic, 2001)

On Hanukkah by Cathy Goldberg Fishman (Atheneum Books for Young Readers, 1998)

One Candle by Eve Bunting (Joanna Cotler Books, 2002)

Festive Farolitos

Light up interest in the nine-day Las Posadas celebration with these colorful and festive farolitos.

Art Concepts
line
pattern
color

Let's Begin

Draw a straight and curvy line on the chalkboard. Ask children to describe each line. Then, invite volunteers to add other kinds of lines, such as zigzag, castle-top, and broken lines. Afterward, show children the completed project. Tell them that it represents a *farolito*—a special kind of light used during the Las Posadas celebration. Ask children to identify the kinds of lines on the project. Are any of the lines repeated? Explain that the series of repeating lines create a pattern. Then, have children identify the colors they see on the project.

Tell children that they will create a colorful paper-bag farolito decorated with a pattern of lines. Pass out the materials and demonstrate the procedures as children follow along.

Materials

To display:
- completed project

For each child:
- white paper bag
- black crayon
- 4½- by 11-inch newspaper pad
- paintbrush

To share:
- watercolor paints (one set for every two children)
- containers of water

Timesaving Tip!

If decorating the front and back of the bag, have children draw the lines on each side before they begin to paint. They can paint one side at a time and then open and stand up the bag to allow the paint to dry.

Step by Step

1. Use a black crayon to draw 6–8 lines across the front of the paper bag. Draw several different types of lines and then repeat the sequence of lines to create a pattern. Leave about 1- to 1½-inches of space between the lines.

2. Slip the newspaper pad into the bag. This will prevent paint from soaking through all layers of the bag.

3. Paint each space between the lines with the watercolor of your choice. You might use only two or three colors to create a color pattern on the bag.

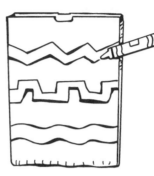

Newspaper

One Step More

Put crumpled newspaper into the bag to help it stand open. Display on a windowsill, bookshelf, or other flat surface in the classroom.

Language Arts Link

Write Spanish and English words related to Las Posadas on the chalkboard. You might include *farolitos*, *luminaries*, *posadas*, *inns*, *pilgrimage*, *peregrinos*, *pilgrims*, *bischochitos*, *cookies*, and *piñata*. Help children count out the syllables as they say each word. Then, have them create a chart to sort the words by syllable count. Invite children to choose words from the chart to use in sentences to demonstrate their knowledge of the Las Posadas celebration. More advanced children might write sentences with the words.

Related Reading

Carlos, Light the Farolito by Jean Ciavonne (Clarion Books, 2001)

Farolitos for Abuelo by Rudolfo Anaya (Hyperion, 1999)

The Farolitos of Christmas by Rudolfo Anaya (Hyperion, 1995)

The Night of Las Posadas by Tomie dePaola (Putnam, 1999)

Fancy Foil-Print Stockings

Use these patterned stockings as a springboard to discuss Christmas-related symbols and traditions.

Art Concepts
shape
texture
pattern

Materials

To display:
- completed project

For each child:
- 9- by 12-inch red construction paper
- scissors
- two 5-inch lengths of aluminum foil
- 3- by 5-inch light green construction paper

To share:
- 12 tagboard stocking templates (page 175)
- pencils
- box of small plastic objects with at least one flat side (soda bottle caps, shape tiles, thread spools, buttons, and so on)
- glue sticks
- color markers

For foil-printing stations:
- shallow trays of white, yellow, and light green tempera paint

Let's Begin

Have children examine the completed project. Tell them that the stocking represents Christmas. Ask them to name other symbols of Christmas.

Then, have them name the colors and shapes in the project. Explain that a pattern is created when one or more elements, such as color and shape, are repeated. Do children see a color or shape pattern on the project? Point out the uneven texture of the prints. Tell children that foil-covered objects were printed onto the stocking to create the texture of the shapes.

Inform children that they will decorate a stocking with a pattern of textured shapes. Pass out the materials and demonstrate the procedures as children follow along.

Timesaving Tip!

Set up three foil-printing stations ahead of time. Cover each table with newspaper, place a paint tray on it, and add a half-inch layer of moist paper towels to each paint tray. Just before beginning the activity, spread a different color paint onto the towels in each tray.

Step by Step

1. Trace the stocking template onto the red construction paper. Cut out the shape.

2. To make a stamper, fold a piece of foil in half. Choose a plastic object from the box and place it flat side down in the center of the foil. Mold the foil around the object and then twist the loose ends together to create a handle. (Don't smooth out the foil as you mold it around the object—the wrinkles that form will help create texture when you print with the stamper.) Make two stampers to use for this project.

Twist to form handle.

Folded foil

Bottle Cap

Mold foil around cap.

3. Take the cutout and foil stampers to the foil-printing stations. Use the stampers to print a simple pattern onto the stocking. You can use the same color to make all the prints, or use a different color for each stamper. Repeat the pattern as often as needed to cover the stocking with foil prints.

4. For the cuff, glue the green construction paper across the top of the stocking. Use markers to write your name on the cuff.

One Step More

Draw and cut out simple pictures of things that would be fun to find in a holiday stocking. Glue the cutouts to the top of the stocking so that it appears to be overflowing with goodies.

Language Arts Link

Tell children that *stocking* begins with the blend *st*. Ask them to brainstorm other words that begin with *st*, such as *star*, *step*, *still*, *stomp*, and *stuck*. List their responses on chart paper. Then, have children use words from the list to make up a class Christmas story. Instruct them to take turns adding to the story so that every child has a chance to contribute. Later, you might challenge more advanced children to write the words from the list in alphabetical order.

Related Reading

Christmas Around the World by Mary Lankford (HarperTrophy, 1998)

The Night Before Christmas by Clement Moore and Bruce Whatley (HarperCollins, 1999)

Santa Who? by Gail Gibbons (HarperCollins, 1999)

Woven-Paper Kwanzaa Mats

Reinforce the traditions and principles of Kwanzaa with these woven-paper mkekas.

Art Concepts

color
line
pattern
shape

Materials

To display:

- completed project

For each child:

- 6- by 9-inch black construction paper
- ruler
- pencil
- scissors
- ten ½- by 9-inch green foil wrapping paper strips
- 12- by 18-inch red construction paper

To share:

- 6 tagboard templates of each shape: circle, square, triangle, rectangle, diamond, and heart (page 176)
- 3-inch squares of green, gold, and silver wrapping paper
- glue sticks

Let's Begin

Show children the completed project and explain that it represents an *mkeka* (em-kay-kah), a straw mat used during the Kwanzaa celebration. Ask children to name the colors on the mat. Tell them that black, red, and green each have a special meaning at Kwanzaa. Then, have them describe the kinds of horizontal and vertical lines they see on the mkeka. Draw their attention to the woven pattern of the mat. Explain that this pattern was created by weaving green strips of paper through the cuts in the black paper. Finally, ask children to identify the foil shapes on the border of the project. Tell them that these shapes were cut from foil wrapping paper.

Let children know that they will create an mkeka by weaving paper. Pass out the materials and demonstrate the procedures as children follow along.

Timesaving Tip!

Use a paper cutter to cut the green foil strips and the 3-inch squares of wrapping paper. You can stack and cut several sheets at a time.

Step by Step

1. Fold the black paper in half horizontally. Use a pencil to draw a vertical line about one ruler width away from the edge opposite the fold. Then, draw four horizontal lines from the fold to the vertical line. You can use straight, curvy, or zigzag lines.

2. Cut along each horizontal line, starting at the fold and stopping at the vertical line. Be sure to cut through both layers of the folded paper. Open the paper to reveal the four horizontal cuts in it.

3. Weave the green paper strips in an over-and-under motion through the horizontal cuts in the black paper. Alternate the weaving pattern for each strip. Slide the strips close together so that they all fit.

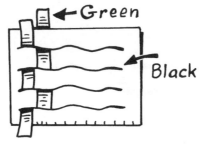

←Green

Black

4. Trim the ends of each paper strip to fit the cutout and glue the ends in place. Glue the woven paper onto the center of the red paper.

5. Trace the shapes of your choice onto the wrapping paper squares. Cut out the shapes and glue them around the border of the woven paper to complete the mkeka.

One Step More

Glue a 2- by 12-inch strip of poster board to the back of one long edge of the mkeka. Punch a hole near each corner, add a yarn hanger, and hang the project on a Kwanzaa-related display.

Language Arts Link

Write *Kwanzaa* on the board and underline the *kw*. Say the word as children listen closely to the beginning sound. Explain that, in English, this sound is spelled with *qu*. Invite children to brainstorm a list of words beginning with *qu*. Write their responses on chart paper. Then, have them write and illustrate alliterative sentences using words from the list (such as "I gave the queen a quarter to quack.") Challenge more advanced children to rewrite each of their sentences as a question or exclamation.

Related Reading

The Gifts of Kwanzaa by Synthia Saint James (Albert Whitman & Co., 1997)

K is for Kwanzaa by Juwanda G. Ford (Scholastic, 1997)

Seven Candles for Kwanzaa by Andrea Davis Pinckney (Puffin Books, 1998)

The Story of Kwanzaa by Donna L. Washington (HarperTrophy, 1997)

Giant New Year Wristwatch

Celebrate the new year and time-telling skills with these giant, colorful watches.

Art Concepts
shape
color

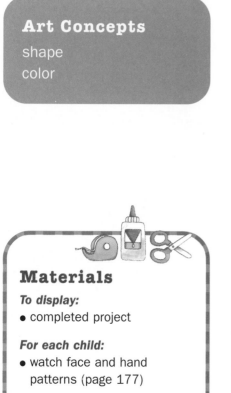

Materials

To display:
- completed project

For each child:
- watch face and hand patterns (page 177)
- pencil
- scissors
- color markers
- brass paper fastener

To share:
- ten 8-inch tagboard circle templates
- 8-inch squares of construction paper in assorted colors
- glue sticks
- 6- by 18-inch strips of construction paper in assorted colors
- scraps of construction paper and foil wrapping paper in assorted sizes and colors

Let's Begin

Show children the completed project. Remind them that the new year starts at 12:00 a.m. on January 1. Invite a volunteer to set the hands on the giant watch to 12:00. Afterward, ask them to name the different colors and shapes used to create the giant watch. Help them identify the different parts of the watch: the face, rim, bands, buckle, and hour and minute hands. Explain that the paper fastener holds the hands in place, but allows them to be moved so that the watch can be set to different times.

Tell children that they will create a giant wristwatch with moveable hands to use for time-telling practice. Pass out the materials and demonstrate the procedures as children follow along.

Timesaving Tip!
Use a paper cutter to cut the squares and strips of construction paper into the sizes needed for the project. You can stack and cut several sheets at a time.

Step by Step

1. Cut out the watch face and the hour and minute hands.

2. Select an 8-inch square of paper in the color of your choice. Trace the 8-inch circle template onto the square. Cut out the circle. Then, glue the watch face to the center of the colored circle to create a rim for the watch.

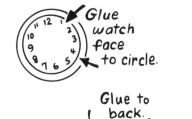

Glue watch face to circle.

3. For the watch band, pick out two 6- by 18-inch strips of construction paper in the color of your choice. Glue one end of each strip to the back of the watch rim, making sure the strips are opposite each other.

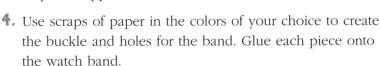

Glue to back.

4. Use scraps of paper in the colors of your choice to create the buckle and holes for the band. Glue each piece onto the watch band.

5. Decorate the watch with drawings or designs of your choice. You might use markers to draw a design or picture on the face. Or you might glue shape cutouts onto the watch to make it resemble a critter or other object. Make sure you don't cover up the numbers on the face.

6. If desired, color the hour and minute hands. Then, use the paper fastener to attach the hands to the watch face. Check to make sure the hands move freely.

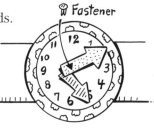

Fastener

One Step More

Display the wristwatches in a line along a wall, making sure they are within easy reach. Have children take turns setting their own watch to a given time.

Language Arts Link

Invite children to tell what time on the clock is their favorite and explain why. For example, they might name the time that a particular activity they enjoy begins or when a favorite TV show airs. Have them write (or dictate) a few sentences about their favorite time and create drawings to go along with their sentences. When finished, ask them to set their giant watches to the corresponding time. Then, display the writings and watches together on a bulletin board. More advanced children might create an illustrated booklet featuring the schedule of their favorite school day of the week. Then, when they share their booklet, they can set their watch to correspond to each time mentioned.

Related Reading

First Night by Harriet Ziefert (Putnam Publishing Group, 1999)

Happy New Year! by Emery Bernhard (Lodestar, 1996)

Happy New Year, Everywhere! by Arlene Erlbach (The Millbrook Press, 2000)

New Year's Day by David F. Marx (Children's Press, 2000)

Chinese New Year Dragon Puppet

Gung Hay Fat Choy! *Introduce children to the customs of the Chinese New Year celebration with these unique dragon puppets.*

Art Concepts
texture
three-dimensional

Materials

To display:
- texture reference chart (page 199)
- completed project

For each child:
- 9- by 10-inch green construction paper
- color markers
- tall chip canister with lid
- two sheets of 9- by 12-inch green construction paper
- pencil
- scissors
- two medium-sized wiggle eyes
- 4- by 7-inch green construction paper

To share:
- glue sticks
- box of scrap paper in assorted colors and sizes (including foil wrapping paper)
- pom-pom balls in assorted colors and sizes
- 12-inch strips of crepe paper streamers in various colors

Let's Begin

Tell children that the Chinese New Year is a 15-day celebration usually held between the middle of January and February. Dragon costumes and puppets are common sights during the parades and festivities. Then, display the completed project and texture reference chart. Point out how the designs drawn on the body make the dragon appear to have texture. Have children describe other kinds of designs that might be used to give texture to the puppet and encourage them to examine the texture reference chart to find similar or other ideas. Finally, explain that the dragon puppet looks more realistic than those seen in pictures because it has three-dimensions—height, width, and depth.

Tell children that they will create a three-dimensional dragon puppet from a chip canister. Pass out the materials and demonstrate the procedures as children follow along.

Timesaving Tip!
Precut 3-inch squares of construction paper and foil wrapping paper for children to use for the facial details.

Step by Step

1. Refer to the texture reference chart to find a design to draw on the dragon to give it texture (or create your own design). Then, place the 9- by 10-inch green paper with the 9-inch side placed vertically on the table. Draw the design on the paper with a marker. To make the dragon's body, glue the paper around the canister.

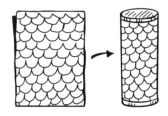

2. Use pencil to draw the outline of a dragon head on a 9- by 12-inch green paper. Use zigzag lines and make the head as large as possible. Cut out the head.

3. Draw the mouth, eye sockets, ears, and other facial details on scrap paper. Cut out the pieces and glue them onto the dragon's head. Add wiggle eyes and pom-pom nostrils. Then, glue the head onto the canister lid and snap the head onto the body.

Glue lid to back of head.

4. Fold the other 9- by 12-inch green paper in half. Use pencil to draw a wing and then cut out the shape through both layers. Add texture and details to the wings. Glue a wing onto each side of the dragon's body.

5. For the tail, cut one end of the 4- by 7-inch green paper to resemble an arrow or spearhead. Add texture and then glue the tail onto the body. Glue a few colorful streamers on the dragon's body at the tail end.

Tail

One Step More

To make a noise-making dragon, put a few dried beans or rice into the canister body before snapping on the dragon head.

Language Arts Link

Ask children to imagine they are a dragon leading the Chinese New Year parade. What sights, sounds, and smells do they experience? Have them write (or dictate) their imaginary experiences on speech bubble cutouts. Use yarn to attach the speech bubbles to the dragons and then display the dragons for children to enjoy. Challenge more advanced children to use and underline adjectives in their writing.

Related Reading

The Dancing Dragon by Marcia K. Vaughan (Mondo Publishing, 1996)

Gung Hay Fat Choy by June Behrens (Children's Press, 1989)

Lanterns and Firecrackers: A Chinese New Year Story by Jonny Zucker (Barron's Educational Series, 2003)

Sam and the Lucky Money by Karen Chinn (Lee & Low Books, 1997)

Warm Winter Jacket

Use these colorful jackets to warm children up to a discussion about weather changes associated with the winter season.

Art Concepts

symmetry
primary colors
secondary colors
complementary colors

Materials

To display:
- color wheel (page 197)
- completed project

For each child:
- 12- by 18-inch red, yellow, or blue construction paper (child's choice)
- pencil
- scissors
- glue stick

To share:
- 12 tagboard jacket templates (page 178)
- scraps of green, orange, and purple construction paper
- assortment of buttons, sequins, ribbons, and lace
- small sticker dots, stars, and other assorted shapes

Let's Begin

Display the color wheel and have children name the six colors on it. Point out the primary colors: red, yellow, and blue. Then, tell children that the other three colors (orange, green, and purple) are secondary colors because they are made by mixing together two primary colors. Continue by pointing out the two colors directly opposite each other on the color wheel: red and green, blue and orange, and yellow and purple. Explain that these are called complementary colors. Next, have children examine the completed project to find the complementary colors. Afterward, draw their attention to the identical shape and features of the two sides of the jacket. Tell children that the jacket is symmetrical because the left side is the mirror image of the right side.

Tell children that they will create a winter jacket using complementary colors. Pass out the materials and demonstrate the procedures as children follow along.

Timesaving Tip!

Precut some scraps of green, orange, and purple construction paper into ½- and 1-inch strips for children to use for the jacket cuffs and bottom band.

Step by Step

1. Fold the 12- by 18-inch sheet of construction paper. Place a jacket template on the paper with the straight edge along the fold. Use a pencil to trace the template. Keeping the paper folded, cut out the shape through both layers. Unfold the cutout to reveal a jacket shape.

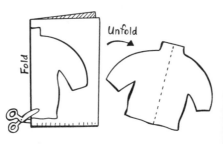

2. Refer to the color wheel to find the complementary color for the color of the jacket cutout. Use scrap paper of this color to create the collar, pocket slits, sleeve cuffs, and bottom band for your jacket. Glue each of these pieces onto the jacket. To make the jacket symmetrical, be sure to glue identical pieces on both sides.

3. Add a line of buttons along one side of the fold line of the jacket. Or, for a zipper, cut a narrow strip of paper in a complementary color, glue it onto the jacket fold, and draw lines along the length of the strip to represent the zipper teeth.

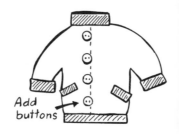

4. Use ribbon, sequins, lace, or stickers to add more decoration to the jacket. Be sure to decorate both sides in the same way so that the jacket is symmetrical in both shape and design.

One Step More

To give texture to the jacket cuffs and bottom band, fan-fold paper strips into narrow folds. Unfold the strips, glue them loosely to the jacket, and trim to fit.

Language Arts Link

Write *jacket* at the top of a sheet of chart paper. Say the word and have children identify the name and sound of the first letter. Then, ask them to brainstorm as many words as possible that begin with *j*, such as *jacket, jar, jelly, jet, juice,* and *jump*. After writing their responses on the chart paper, review the words with the class. Say one word at a time, some beginning with *j* and others beginning with other sounds. Ask children to jump three times each time they hear a *j* word. Have more advanced children write each *j* word after they complete their jumps.

Related Reading

Coat of Many Colors by Dolly Parton (HarperTrophy, 1996)

A New Coat for Anna by Harriet Ziefert (Dragonfly Books, 1988)

The Purple Coat by Amy Hest (Aladdin, 1992)

The Rag Coat by Lauren A. Mills (Little, Brown Young Readers, 1991)

Marvelous Mittens

These personalized projects can be used as a springboard to explore how mittens warm and protect hands in cold, wintry weather.

Art Concepts

line
color
pattern
symmetry

Materials

To display:
- completed project

For each child:
- two 9- by 12-inch sheets of light construction paper in the same color
- pencil
- scissors
- fine-tip black permanent marker

To share:
- 15 tagboard mitten templates (page 179)
- oil pastels (one box for every two children)

Let's Begin

Display the completed project. Ask children to examine the mittens and describe the kinds of lines they see on them. Do any lines repeat on the mittens? Next, have them name the colors on the mittens. Are there any repeating colors? Highlight the line and color patterns on the mitten pair. Then, have children compare the two mittens to each other. What similarities do they see? After sharing their observations, point out that both mittens are decorated with the same line and color patterns. Explain that the mittens are mirror images of each other—they are symmetrical in shape and design.

Tell children that they will design and create a pair of symmetrical mittens. Pass out the materials and demonstrate the procedures as children follow along.

Timesaving Tip!

Ask every two children to share a mitten template. Have the children take turns tracing and cutting out one mitten at a time.

Step by Step

1. Use a pencil to trace a mitten template onto both of the 9- by 12-inch sheets of paper. Cut out each shape.

2. Pencil in a set of parallel lines near the finger end of a mitten. Use a straight, curvy, zigzag, or castle-top line design, or any other type of line of your choice. Be sure to draw the lines about one-half to one inch apart.

3. Draw another pair of parallel lines about one inch from the first set. Then, add a third and fourth set of parallel lines. You might use different kinds of lines for each set.

4. Draw a straight line to section off the cuff at the wrist end of the mitten. Fill in that section with the design of your choice.

5. Position the other mitten on the table with the thumb touching the thumb of the first mitten. Then, using the first mitten as a guide, draw the same lines and designs onto the second mitten. When finished, you'll have a matching left and right mitten.

6. Trace all the lines with the black marker. Then, use oil pastels in the colors of your choice to color both mittens so that they match.

One Step More

Connect the pair of mittens by taping each end of a 12-inch length of yarn to the back of a mitten.

Language Arts Link

Tell children that a pair of mittens is made up of a right and left mitten. Explain that *right* and *left* are opposites. Invite them to name other opposites such as *top/bottom, front/back,* and *big/little.* Write their responses on the chalkboard. Then, ask children to select five opposite pairs from the list to illustrate on separate sheets of paper. Have them write the opposite pair for each picture, staple the pages between two construction-paper covers, and then title the booklet "My Opposites Book." Challenge more advanced children to include ten opposite pairs in their booklets and to write sentences describing the opposite relationship of the items in their drawings.

Related Reading

Missing Mittens by Stuart J. Murphy (HarperTrophy, 2000)

The Mitten by Jan Brett (Putnam, 1989)

The Mitten Tree by Candace Christiansen (Fulcrum Publishing, 1997)

One Mitten by Kristine O'Connell George (Clarion, 2004)

Torn-Paper Winter Wear

Invite children to use these torn-paper projects as they discuss ways to dress warmly on cold winter days.

Art Concepts
shape
torn paper

Materials

To display:
● completed project

For each child:
● 3- by 12-inch white construction paper
● 9- by 12-inch black construction paper
● pencil

To share:
● 3-inch squares of paper in various flesh tones and assorted colors
● glue sticks
● fine-tip black permanent markers

Let's Begin

Talk with children about some outdoor, snowy day activities such as building snowmen, sledding, snowboarding, and making snow angels. Then, ask them to name some kinds of clothing they might wear to stay warm in cold, snowy weather. Their responses might include hats, mittens, scarves, boots, snow pants, and coats. Afterward, show children the completed project. Have them name the colors and shapes in the picture. Can they identify the different types of clothing? Tell them that all the pieces in the picture were made from paper torn into different shapes and sizes. Explain that the torn edges of the shapes give the picture a fuzzy, but realistic appearance—similar to the way a scene looks when snow is falling.

Tell children that they will tear paper into shapes to create their own snowy day pictures. Pass out the materials and demonstrate the procedures as children follow along.

TimeSaving Tip!
Use a paper cutter to cut the construction paper into the sizes needed for the project. You can stack and cut several sheets at a time.

Step by Step

1. Tear small pieces off one long edge of the 3- by 12-inch white paper. Glue the strip to the bottom edge of the black paper so that it looks like a layer of snow on the ground.

2. For the coat, choose a 3-inch paper square in the color of your choice. Tear a strip from two opposite sides of the square. Glue the two strips onto the larger piece to create a coat with sleeves. Tear a narrow strip from the bottom of the coat for use as a scarf. Glue the coat to the center of the black paper.

3. Tear out a head from a flesh-colored square of paper. Glue the head to the top of the coat, slightly overlapping the pieces. Glue the scarf onto the picture.

Scarf

4. Choose another paper square for the pants. Tear small pieces away from two opposite sides of the square to make the edges uneven. Then, tear the square in half. Glue each piece, or leg, onto the picture so that it slightly overlaps the bottom edge of the coat.

5. For boots, choose two paper squares in the same color. Lightly pencil in a block "L" with rounded corners on one square. Then, stack the squares, tear out the shape through both layers, and glue a boot-shaped piece to the bottom of each leg. Repeat to make mittens. Glue each mitten to the end of a coat sleeve.

6. Tear out a triangle hat from a paper square. Glue the hat onto the head. Use a marker to add facial features and other details.

One Step More

Add a torn-paper sled, snowman, or other snow-related item to the picture. Then, glue on torn-paper snowflakes to represent falling snow.

Language Arts Link

Write *winter* and *wear* on the chalkboard. Ask children to tell what the two words have in common. After noting that both start with *w*, have them brainstorm other words that begin with *w*, such as *walrus, wheel, wig, woman,* and *worm.* List their responses on the board. Then, invite children to create "My Wonderful World of W Words" posters. Have them draw or glue cutouts of pictures that begin with *w* and then label each picture with the corresponding word. Challenge more advanced children to group the words on their posters by the parts of speech they represent: nouns, verbs, or adjectives.

Related Reading

Emmett's Snowball by Ned Miller (Henry Holt Young Readers, 1996)

The Jacket I Wear in the Snow by Shirley Neitzel (HarperTrophy, 1994)

The Snowy Day by Ezra Jack Keats (Puffin, 1976)

Tracks in the Snow by Wong Herbert Yee (Henry Holt and Co., 2003)

Snowflake Banner

Use these pretty banners to explore and discuss the characteristics of snowflakes.

Art Concepts
shape

pattern

contrasting colors

positive and negative
   space

Materials

To display:
- pictures of snowflakes (see Related Reading for books featuring snowflake pictures)
- completed project

For each child:
- 9- by 12-inch white construction paper
- six 3-inch squares of purple construction paper
- 3-inch circles of blue and white bulletin board paper (six of each color)
- pencil
- scissors

To share:
- glue sticks

Let's Begin

Display pictures of snowflakes and the completed project. Discuss the six-sided shape and other characteristics of snowflakes. Then, have children describe the similarities and differences between the pictures of snowflakes and the snowflakes on the banner. Afterward, point out the pattern created by the snowflakes and colors on the banner. Tell children that when dark and light colors are put together, they are called contrasting colors. Have them name the contrasting colors on the project. Inform children that the space occupied by each snowflake is positive space while the area surrounding it is negative space.

Tell children that they will make a snowflake banner using contrasting colors. Pass out the materials and demonstrate the procedures as children follow along.

Timesaving Tip!

To prepare the circles, cut the blue and white paper into 3-inch squares. Then, trace around a 15-ounce soup can or chip canister lid onto a stack of squares. Cut out the circle through all layers.

Step by Step

1. Place the white paper horizontally on the table. Glue a purple square in the top and bottom corner on the left side of the paper. Using these squares as a guide, glue the other purple squares onto the paper to create a checkerboard pattern.

2. Stack and fold three white circles in half. Then, fold the half-circle into thirds. Use a pencil to draw one or more simple figures (such as triangles) along a straight side of the folded circles. Start and finish drawing each figure on the fold, leaving some space between each one. Continue by drawing figures along the other straight side and the curved edge of the folded circles.

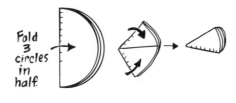

Fold 3 circles in half.

3. Carefully cut out the figures through all layers. Unfold the circles to reveal a snowflake shape. Gently separate the three snowflakes.

4. Cut out a second set of snowflakes by repeating Steps 2 and 3 with the remaining three white circles. Then, cut snowflakes from the blue circles.

5. Position the white snowflakes onto the purple squares of the checkerboard paper to create a pattern. Then, glue on the snowflakes. Repeat with the blue snowflakes by gluing them in a pattern onto the white squares.

One Step More

Glue the banner to a 12- by 18-inch sheet of blue or purple construction paper. Display the banners in a line across the top of a long wall to create a snowy border.

Language Arts Link

Create a chart with the headings "One Syllable," "Two Syllables," and "Three Syllables." Then, have children name snow-related words such as *snowflake, snowball, shower, shiver, melt, freeze, cold,* and so on. As a class, decide how many syllables each word contains. Invite a volunteer to write each word in the corresponding column on the chart. For more advanced children, write a list of snow-related words on chart paper. Ask children to work individually to create a chart and then copy the words onto the chart to show the syllable count of each word on the list.

Related Reading

Snow Is Falling by Stuart J. Murphy (HarperTrophy, 2000)

Snowflake Bentley by Jacqueline Briggs Martin (Houghton Mifflin, 1998)

Snowflakes in Photographs by W. A. Bentley (Dover Publications, 2000)

Snowy Winter Scene

These snowy scenes make a great discussion-starter about how the seasonal weather of winter can change the landscape of your community.

Art Concepts
overlap
texture
pattern

Materials

To display:
- pictures of snow-covered landscapes
- completed project

For each child:
- 9- by 12-inch blue construction paper
- white chalk
- oil pastels

To share:
- scraps of gold foil wrapping paper
- scissors
- glue sticks

For paint-printing station:
- twelve 1-inch square sponges
- shallow trays of white tempera paint
- 12 wooden pencils with erasers

Let's Begin

Display the pictures of snow-covered landscapes. Explain that when snow falls it covers the ground, roofs, tree limbs, and many other objects. Ask children to describe how the scene might have looked before the snow fell. Then, show them the completed project. Point out how the overlapping buildings and objects give the scene a more realistic appearance. Tell children that the uneven coloring of the snow on the objects was created with sponge prints. This technique gives the snow a textured appearance and makes it seem more realistic. Finally, point out that the falling snow was created by repeating a pattern of sponge prints and pencil eraser prints.

Tell children that they will create a snowy winter scene of their own community. Pass out the materials and demonstrate the procedures as children follow along.

Timesaving Tip!

Set up a paint-printing station ahead of time. Cover a table with newspaper. Add a half-inch layer of moist paper towels to several paint trays. Then, place the trays, sponges, and pencils on the table. Just before beginning the activity, spread white paint onto the towels in each tray.

Step by Step

1. Place the 9- by 12-inch blue paper horizontally on the table. Use chalk to draw a horizontal line about three finger widths above the bottom edge of the paper. This line represents the ground for your picture.

2. Using chalk, sketch the buildings, trees, and other objects in your scene. As you draw, use an overlapping technique so that some objects (such as buildings) are partially hidden by other objects (such as trees).

Chalk

3. Trace the chalk drawing with a black oil pastel. Then, color the picture using pastels in the colors of your choice.

4. Cut out gold foil shapes to glue onto objects, such as the moon, windows, and street lamps, so that they appear to glow with light.

5. Take the project to the paint-printing station. Use sponge-prints to cover the ground, roofs, tree tops, and other objects with a layer of snow. Press the sponge lightly onto the picture to avoid printing a heavy coat of paint onto the objects.

6. For falling snow, sponge-print snowflakes randomly across your picture. Then, add eraser-print snowflakes to represent individual snowflakes.

white
Sponge

One Step More

Create a wintry background by covering a bulletin board with sheets of snow felt. Then, attach the snowy winter scenes to the display.

Language Arts Link

Tell children that *snowy* begins with the blend *sn*. Ask them to brainstorm other words that begin with *sn*, such as *snack*, *sneak*, *snip*, *snore*, and *snug*. List their responses on chart paper. Then, have children use words from the list to make up a class wintry day story. Instruct them to take turns adding to the story so that every child has a chance to contribute. Later, you might challenge more advanced children to sort the words from the list by vowel types (such as long, short, and *r*-controlled) and then by the specific vowel sounds.

Related Reading

Names for Snow by Judith K. Beach (Hyperion, 2003)

Snow Music by Lynne Rae Perkins (Greenwillow, 2003)

Dear Rebecca, Winter Is Here by Jean Craighead George (HarperTrophy, 1995)

Snowman Puzzle

Use these snowmen puzzles to review the solid and liquid properties of snow.

Art Concepts

shape
line
pattern

Materials

To display:
- completed project

For each child:
- 9- by 12-inch white construction paper
- pencil
- scissors
- 12- by 18-inch blue construction paper
- 4½- by 6-inch white construction paper

To share:
- glue sticks
- scraps of different kinds of paper in assorted colors (construction paper, stationery, wrapping paper, and so on)

Let's Begin

Draw a straight and curvy line on the chalkboard and ask children to describe each line. Invite volunteers to add other kinds of lines, such as zigzag, castle-top, and broken lines. Afterward, show children the completed project. Have them describe the shapes and colors used in the puzzle. Then, point out the lines that divide the snowman puzzle into separate pieces. What kind of lines were used? Explain that the lines create a pattern because they are repeated throughout the puzzle. To conclude, point out that a real snowman is made of snow, which is water in its solid form. What form does snow take when it melts? Invite children to share their experiences with building snowmen and watching them melt.

Tell children that they will use shapes and lines to create a snowman puzzle. Pass out the materials and demonstrate the procedures as children follow along.

Timesaving Tip!

Precut assorted colors of scrap paper into circles, triangles, narrow rectangles, and squares for children to use for their snowman features.

Step by Step

1. For the snowman's body, use pencil to draw a large circle or oval on the 9- by 12-inch white paper. Cut out the shape, then draw four or five lines across the shape to make your puzzle. You might use straight, curvy, or zigzag lines or any other line type of your choice. Try to leave the same amount of space between each line. Cut along the lines to create the puzzle pieces for the body.

2. Place the 12- by 18-inch blue construction paper vertically on the table. Assemble the pieces of the body at the bottom of the paper, leaving a little space between each piece. Then, glue the pieces in place.

3. For the head, repeat Step 1 using the 4½- by 6-inch white paper. Then, assemble the puzzle pieces for the head above the body. Glue the pieces in place.

4. Cut out facial features, arms, clothing items, and other snowman details from scraps of colored paper. Glue the details onto the puzzle snowman.

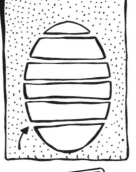

One Step More

Use a piece of white chalk or oil pastel to draw background details and falling snow on the blue paper.

Language Arts Link

Write *puzzle*, and have children name the sound they hear in the middle of the word. Ask them to name other words that contain the *z* sound, such as *zipper*, *dizzy*, and *jazz*. List their responses on chart paper. If they name a word in which the *z* sound is spelled with a letter other than *z* (such as in *busy*), write this word at the bottom of the chart. Then, underline the letter that makes the *z* sound in each word. Help children organize the words into three separate lists according to where *z* is heard in each word: the beginning, middle, or end. More advanced children can write and illustrate alliterative sentences using words with the *z* sound.

Related Reading

All You Need for a Snowman by Alice Schertle (Silver Whistle, 2002)

Snowmen at Night by Caralyn Buehner (Dial, 2002)

The Snowman by Raymond Briggs (Random House Books for Young Readers, 1978)

The Biggest, Best Snowman by Margerie Cuyler (Scholastic, 2004)

Glistening Snow Globe

Encourage children to use their snow globes to share what they know about the role of snow in the water cycle.

Art Concepts
color
shape
overlap

Materials

To display:
- completed project

For each child:
- 8-inch light blue construction paper circle
- pencil
- scissors
- crayons
- glue stick
- 8-inch circle cut from clear transparency film (or page protectors)
- 8-inch white construction paper circle
- 4- by 6-inch brown construction paper

To share:
- scraps of construction paper in assorted colors, including white
- hole punches (one for every four children)
- small foil star stickers (optional)
- twelve 7-inch tagboard circles

Let's Begin

Display the completed project. Explain to children that the project is a model of a snow globe. Many snow globes contain a miniature outdoor scene inside a clear glass or plastic bubble filled with water. When shaken, white particles representing snowflakes float through the water and drift to the bottom of the globe. Ask children to name the colors and shapes used to create the snow globe. Point out how the overlapping figures in the globe help give the scene a more realistic appearance. Then, tell them that the falling snow is made from white hole-punch holes. To conclude, explain the role of snow in the water cycle.

Tell children that they will create a snow globe. Pass out the materials and demonstrate the procedures as children follow along.

TimeSaving Tip!

To cut out the 8-inch circles, stack together a sheet of white paper, transparency film, and light blue paper, in that order. Put two stacks together, draw the circle on the top sheet, and cut out the circle through all layers.

Step by Step

1. Use pencil to draw a horizontal line about three finger widths above the bottom rim of the light blue circle. This will be the ground line for your scene.

2. On scraps of paper, use pencil to draw simple pictures of things for your scene (such as a snowman, tree, puppy, house, and so on). Cut out the pictures. Use crayons to add details, such as facial features and windowpanes. Glue the cutouts onto the blue circle to create a scene. Overlap some of the objects to make the scene look more realistic.

3. For snowflakes, use the hole punch to punch holes from white paper scraps. Glue the snowflakes onto the scene. If desired, add a few star stickers.

4. Glue the clear circle over the scene, gluing only around the rim of the circle.

5. Center and trace a 7-inch tagboard circle onto the 8-inch white circle. Cut along the outline to remove the inside circle from the larger white circle. When finished, you'll have a large white ring. Glue the ring onto the scene so that it creates a frame.

Glue to snow globe.

6. For the base, trim the 4- by 6-inch brown paper into a trapezoid shape, or any other shape of your choice. Use a black crayon to draw a simple design on the base. Then, glue the snow globe onto the base, overlapping the top of the base with the bottom rim of the globe.

One Step More

Attach each snow globe to a tall chip canister. Then, display the stand-up projects on a windowsill, bookshelf, or other flat surface.

Language Arts Link

Tell children that *glistening* and *globe* begin with the blend *gl*. Ask them to brainstorm other words that begin with *gl*, such as *glad, glass, glitter, glob, glow,* and *glum*. List their responses on chart paper. Have children use words from the list to make up serious and silly sentences. Invite them to write and illustrate their sentences on paper. More advanced children might illustrate each word on a half-sheet of paper and then alphabetize and staple the pages together to create a picture dictionary of *gl* words.

Related Reading

The Snow Globe Family by Jane O'Connor (Putnam Juvenile, 2006)

When It Starts to Snow by Phillis Gershator (Henry Holt and Co., 2001)

Sponge-Print Penguins

*Invite children to show off these sponge-print critters
as they share their penguin knowledge with others.*

Art Concepts
shape
texture
overlap

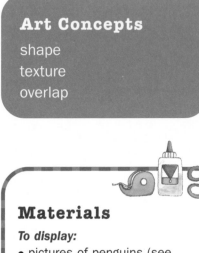

Materials

To display:
- pictures of penguins (see Related Reading for books featuring penguin pictures)
- completed project

For each child:
- 12- by 18-inch blue construction paper
- pencil
- 9- by 12-inch black construction paper
- scissors
- 3-inch square of black construction paper
- 3-inch square of orange construction paper

To share:
- glue sticks
- scraps of assorted paper in different colors and designs (foil and embossed wrapping paper, wallpaper, stationery, and so on)

For sponge-printing station:
- twelve 1-inch square sponges
- shallow trays of white tempera paint

Let's Begin

Use the penguin pictures to review different features and characteristics of these cold-weather birds. Then, show children the completed project. Call their attention to the shapes used in the project and how they compare to the shapes seen in the bird pictures. Point out how the white sponge prints on the front of the penguin's body give it a feathery-looking texture. Tell children that the overlapping body parts help give the penguin a more realistic appearance.

Inform children that they will create a sponge-print penguin. Pass out the materials and demonstrate the procedures as children follow along.

Timesaving Tip!

Set up a sponge-printing station ahead of time. Cover a table with newspaper. Add a half-inch layer of moist paper towels to several paint trays and place the trays and sponges on the table. Just before beginning the activity, spread white paint onto the towels in each tray.

Step by Step

1. To make the body, use pencil to draw a large oval on the 12- by 18-inch blue paper. For the feathers, take the paper to the sponge-printing station to fill in the shape with white sponge prints. Press the sponges lightly onto the shape, overlapping the prints to achieve a soft, feathery effect.

Sponge

2. For the wings (or flippers), fold the 9- by 12-inch black paper in half vertically. Draw a large half-oval, starting at the long open end of the paper. Cut out the shape through both layers. Overlap the left side of the body with one wing and the right side with the other wing. (Trim the wings to a smaller size if needed.) Glue each one in place.

Fold

Two oval wings

3. Round out the corners of the 3-inch black square to make the head. Place the head so that it overlaps the top of the body. Glue the head onto the body.

4. To make feet, fold the 3-inch orange paper in half. Draw a foot and then cut out the shape through both layers. Glue the feet to the bottom of the body.

5. Draw other body parts on scrap paper in the colors of your choice. You might also draw a hat, scarf, or ear muffs. Cut out each piece and glue it onto the penguin.

One Step More

Use a black marker to add background scenery to the areas of the paper surrounding the penguin.

Language Arts Link

Tell children that penguins are surrounded by ice at their Antarctic home. Write *ice* on the chalkboard. Ask children to name other words that belong to the same word family, such as *mice, nice, price, rice, slice,* and *twice.* Write each word on the board. Call on volunteers to complete the sentence "My penguin lives on ice, and he..." with a funny or serious phrase that ends with a word from the *-ice* word family. Ask more advanced children to use the word family words to write a short rhyme or create words to sing to the tune of familiar songs.

Related Reading

The Emperor's Egg: Read and Wonder by Martin Jenkins (Candlewick, 2002)

Penguin Chick by Betty Tatham (HarperTrophy, 2001)

Penguin (Watch Me Grow) by DK Publishing (2004)

Plenty of Penguins by Sonia Black (Cartwheel, 2000)

Arms of Friendship

After learning about Dr. Martin Luther King, Jr., children can use these special arms to share their own message of peace and friendship.

Art Concepts

shape
color
pattern

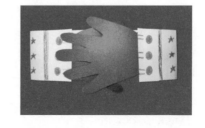

Materials

To display:
- completed project

For each child:
- 4- by 24-inch white construction paper
- crayons
- scissors
- 4- by 8-inch white construction paper

To share:
- glue sticks
- 6- by 9-inch construction paper in assorted flesh colors

Let's Begin

Invite children to share what they know about Dr. Martin Luther King, Jr. and the national holiday named after him. After discussing his message of peace and friendship, display the completed project. Unfold the hands and help children read the message on the cloud. Then, ask them to name the shapes and colors on the sleeves. (Be sure to show them both sides of the sleeves.) Explain that a pattern is made when a shape or design is repeated. Do children see any patterns on the sleeve? Encourage them to share their observations. Point out that the pattern on the cuff differs from the pattern on the outer sleeve, but it matches the pattern on the inside of the sleeve.

Tell children that they will create an arms of friendship project that contains their own message of peace or friendship. Pass out the materials and demonstrate the procedures as children follow along.

Timesaving Tip!

Ask children to trace only one hand in Step 3. Then, have them stack another sheet of paper behind the tracing, cut out the shape through both layers, and use the two hand cutouts in their project.

Step by Step

1. To make sleeves, use crayons to decorate one side of the 4- by 24-inch white paper with a repeating pattern of shapes or designs. You might use shapes such as squares, circles, and stars or designs such as stripes, dots, and swirls. Or you might use a combination of shapes and designs. When finished, turn the paper strip over and decorate the back with a different pattern.

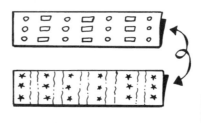

2. Fold about 1½ inch of each end of the sleeve strip toward the middle to create cuffs. Glue the cuffs in place.

3. Choose two 6- by 9-inch papers in the same flesh color. Use pencil to trace each hand onto a sheet of the paper. You might ask a friend to trace your writing hand for you. Cut out both hands. Glue each hand, with the thumb facing up, to an end of the sleeve strip.

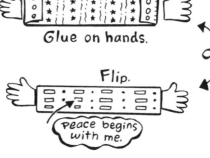
Glue on hands.

4. Turn the sleeve strip over. Then, cut the 4- by 8-inch white paper into a cloud shape. Write a message about friendship or peace on the shape. Glue the message onto the middle of the sleeve strip.

Flip.
Peace begins with me.

5. Fold each hand toward the middle so that they overlap and cover the message. Invite your friends to unfold the hands to read your special message.

One Step More

Display the arms of friendship around a bulletin board or across a long wall. Leave the hands loose so that they fall open and the message is visible for all to read.

Language Arts Link

Remind children that Dr. King is well-known for his "I Have a Dream" speech. Invite children to share what kind of dreams they might have to make their world a more peaceful place to live. Afterward, have them cut out large dream bubbles, write (or dictate) a sentence or two about their dream, and then illustrate their sentences. Encourage more advanced children to write a paragraph about their dream on one side of the dream bubble and then illustrate the other side.

Related Reading

Happy Birthday, Martin Luther King by Jean Marzolla (Scholastic, 1993)

Martin's Big Words: The Life of Martin Luther King, Jr. by Doreen Rappaport (Jump at the Sun, 2001)

My Dream of Martin Luther King by Faith Ringgold (Dragonfly Books, 1998)

Origami Groundhog Mask

Encourage children to use these unique masks as they learn about groundhogs and explore light and shadows.

Art Concepts

origami
shape
texture

Materials

To display:
- completed project
- 12-inch square of light brown construction paper
- texture reference chart (page 199)

For each child:
- 12-inch square of light brown construction paper
- pencil
- scissors
- two 3-inch squares of light brown construction paper
- black, brown, yellow, and red crayons

To share:
- glue sticks
- 12 plastic soda bottle caps

Let's Begin

Show children the completed project. Invite them to share their ideas about what animal the mask represents. Afterward, tell them that the project is a groundhog mask. Show them the light brown paper square, and have them identify the shape. Explain that the mask was made from the same size square using a paper-folding technique called origami. Call children's attention to the short lines that fill up the front of the mask. Tell them that the lines create a furry-looking texture that gives the mask a more realistic appearance. Have children examine the texture reference chart to find a similar or other designs that have the appearance of fur.

Inform children that they will follow a step-by-step lesson in origami to make a groundhog mask. Pass out the materials and have children follow each step as you demonstrate how to fold the paper and make the mask.

Timesaving Tip!

Use a paper cutter to cut the light brown construction paper into 12-inch squares. You can stack and cut several sheets at a time.

Step by Step

1. Fold the 12-inch square of brown paper in half diagonally. Unfold the paper and turn it so that it looks like a diamond on the table. Fold the bottom left and right corners toward the center fold line so that you have a kite shape.

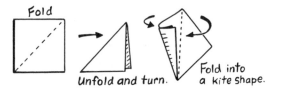

2. Draw a 2-inch line across the center fold line, as shown. Carefully cut along the line. Insert the bottom tip of the "kite" through the slit as far as it will go, then fold the tip down on the other side—or front—of the mask. To make the nose, fold the tip under and toward the slit and glue in place. Trim the top of the mask to round off the head.

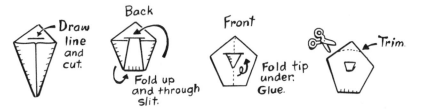

3. For the eye holes, trace the soda bottle cap about one inch away from the center fold line and above the nose drawing a circle on the left and right sides of the center line. Cut out each eye hole.

4. Cut out ears from the two 3-inch squares of brown paper. Glue an ear onto each side of the mask.

5. Color the nose black and draw a mouth on the mask. Use the brown and yellow crayons to draw fur on the mask, including the ears.

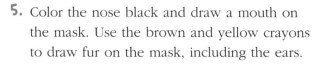

One Step More

To make a handle, glue a wide craft stick to the bottom of the mask.

Language Arts Link

Explain that according to tradition, if the groundhog sees its shadow on Groundhog Day, it will rush back into its burrow, and there will be six more weeks of winter. Write *shadow* on the left side of a sheet of chart paper and *rush* on the right side. Say the two words, point out the *sh* in each one, and discuss its position in the word. Then, have children name words that begin or end with *sh* (such as *shack, shell, hush,* and *wish*). Invite volunteers to write the words under *shadow* or *hush,* according to where *sh* is heard in the word. Afterward, invite more advanced children to create groundhog-related skits using as many *sh* words as possible. They can use their masks to perform the skits for the class.

Related Reading

A Garden for a Groundhog by Lornia Balian (Star Bright Books, 2003)

Geoffrey Groundhog Predicts the Weather by Bruce Koscielniak (Houghton Mifflin, 1998)

Will Spring Be Early? Or Will Spring Be Late? by Crockett Johnson (HarperTrophy, 1990)

Valentine Bear Puppet

Invite children to use these cute bears to deliver Valentine's Day greetings and special messages to their friends and family.

Art Concepts

shape
symmetry
three-dimensional

Materials

To display:
- completed project

For each child:
- small white paper bag
- 4- by 6-inch pink construction paper
- four 3- by 4-inch sheets of hot pink construction paper
- pencil
- two 2-inch squares of hot pink construction paper
- scissors
- 3-inch square of red construction paper

To share:
- glue sticks
- 12 tagboard paw templates (page 180)
- 12 tagboard ear templates (page 180)
- 6 tagboard heart templates in each size (page 180)
- scraps of paper in Valentine's Day colors and patterns (construction paper, wrapping paper, wallpaper samples, and so on)
- red or black markers

Let's Begin

Ask children to examine the completed project. What animal and special day does it represent? Have them name the shapes and colors used to make the bear puppet. Then, call their attention to the identical shapes and features on each side of the puppet. Tell children that the bear is symmetrical because the left side is the mirror image of the right side. Explain that the puppet also has three-dimensions—height, width, and depth—which helps give it a more realistic appearance.

Tell children that they will make a Valentine bear puppet from a paper bag. Pass out the materials and demonstrate the procedures as children follow along.

Timesaving Tip!

In step 2, ask children to trace a paw template onto one 3- by 4-inch sheet of hot pink paper. Then, have them stack the other hot pink papers behind it, cut out the shape through all layers, and use the four paw cutouts for their project.

Step by Step

1. Place the bag on the table with the bottom facing up and the open end closest to you. Glue the 4- by 6-inch pink paper onto the bag bottom. This will be the bear's head.

2. In pencil, trace a paw template on each of the 3- by 4-inch sheets of hot pink paper. Cut out each paw and then add paw pads with a marker. Glue a paw onto each side of the bag to represent arms. For legs, glue the other two paws onto the bag at the open end.

3. Use the pencil to trace the ear template on the two 2-inch squares of hot pink paper. Cut out and glue the ears to the head.

4. For the muzzle, use pencil to draw a large circle on the 3-inch red paper square. Cut out the circle and glue it onto the head. Use a marker to draw a nose, mouth, and eyes on the bear.

5. Choose several pieces of scrap paper. Trace a heart template onto each piece. You might use the same or different size heart on each one. Cut out the hearts and glue them onto your puppet. Then, slip your hand into the puppet and use it to tell others your special Valentine's Day messages.

One Step More

Write a special Valentine's Day message on a white speech bubble cutout. Attach the bubble near the bear's mouth.

Language Arts Link

Have small groups of children create short skits about friendship and rehearse the skits using their puppets. They might write (or dictate) their speaking parts on strips of paper to help them remember what to say. Invite each group to perform its skit for the class. Challenge more advanced children to write out their entire skits. After performing the skit, they can give the script to other groups to read and perform.

Related Reading

The Day It Rained Hearts by Felicia Bond (Laura Geringer, 2001)

The Night Before Valentine's Day by Natasha Wing (Grosset & Dunlap, 2001)

Roses Are Pink, Your Feet Really Stink by Diane deGroat (HarperTrophy, 1997)

The Valentine Bears by Eve Bunting (Clarion Books, 1985)

Puffy Presidential License Plate

Review the roles and responsibilities of our nation's President with these stuffed license plates.

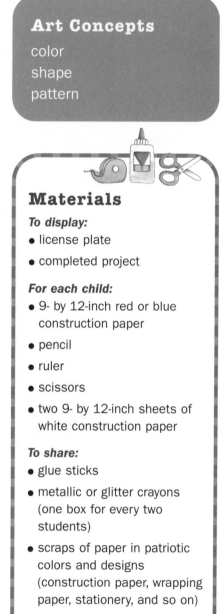

Art Concepts
color
shape
pattern

Materials

To display:
- license plate
- completed project

For each child:
- 9- by 12-inch red or blue construction paper
- pencil
- ruler
- scissors
- two 9- by 12-inch sheets of white construction paper

To share:
- glue sticks
- metallic or glitter crayons (one box for every two students)
- scraps of paper in patriotic colors and designs (construction paper, wrapping paper, stationery, and so on)
- party confetti in patriotic shapes and colors (available at craft stores)
- foil star stickers
- white tissue paper (or newspaper)

Let's Begin

Have children examine and compare the license plate and completed project. Tell them that some people order customized license plates featuring numbers, letters, symbols, or pictures that have special meaning to them. Then, have children identify the colors, shapes, and patterns on the project. Ask them to tell what person the license plate might represent. After sharing, explain that the plate represents the President of the United States. Talk about the colors and symbols associated with the presidency (such as an eagle, the American flag, Air Force One, and so on). Point out any of these that are featured on the project. Finally, tell children that the license plate was stuffed with paper to give it a puffy appearance.

Tell children that they will create a customized presidential license plate. Pass out the materials and demonstrate the procedures as children follow along.

Timesaving Tip!

To precut the frame in Step 1, stack and fold several sheets of paper together, draw the cutting lines, and then cut along the lines through all layers of paper.

Step by Step

1. Fold the 9- by 12-inch colored paper in half horizontally. Use a ruler and pencil to draw a line about 1½ inch away from each of the three open

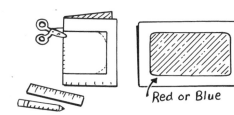

Red or Blue

edges of the paper. Round out the corners where the lines meet. Then, starting and ending at the fold, cut along the lines. Unfold the paper to reveal a frame.

2. Glue the frame to a 9- by 12-inch sheet of white paper. Cut through both layers to round each outer corner of the frame.

3. In the white section of the license plate, use crayons to draw a picture, symbol, or pattern to represent the presidency. Or draw shapes on a few paper scraps, cut out the shapes, and glue them to the plate.

Decorate frame and white area.

4. Decorate the license plate frame with star stickers, stripes, confetti, lettering, or other designs of your choice.

5. Back the license plate with the other 9- by 12-inch sheet of white paper. Glue the bottom and side edges together, leaving the top edge open. Crumple and stuff tissue paper into the opening. Then, glue the top edges together.

Stuff with paper.

One Step More

To display, punch a hole in the top corners of the license plate. Then, tie each end of an 18-inch length of yarn to a hole to create a hanger.

Language Arts Link

Read *If I Were President* by Catherine Stier (see Related Reading). Then, ask children to imagine they are the President. Invite them to share their favorite imaginary experiences of the office. Afterward, have them create and label a mini-poster to highlight a specific job performed by the President. Have more advanced children create mini-booklets that feature different jobs of the President.

Related Reading

If I Were President by Catherine Stier (Albert Whitman & Company, 2004)

My Teacher for President by Kay Winters (Dutton Juvenile, 2004)

So You Want to Be President? by Judith St. George (Philomel, 2004)

Woodrow, the White House Mouse by Peter W. Barnes (Vacation Spot, 1998)

In the Style of Vincent Van Gogh: Night Lights

*Have children create these masterpieces as they explore
the technique, moods, and colors of Van Gogh's art.*

Art Concepts

landscape
horizon
shape
overlap

Materials

To display:
- *Starry Night* by Vincent Van Gogh (page 203)
- completed project

For each child:
- 12- by 18-inch blue construction paper
- white chalk

To share:
- oil pastels (one box for every two children)

For watercolor paint station:
- purple watercolor paints
- wide or chubby paintbrushes
- containers of water

Let's Begin

Tell children that Vincent Van Gogh is famous for works such as *Starry Night*. Show them the print of the painting, and explain that *Starry Night* is called a landscape because it pictures a natural outdoor scene. Then, call their attention to the horizon—the line where the sky and land appear to meet. Ask children to name some of the shapes Van Gogh used to create trees, houses, and other objects. Do any of the objects overlap? Explain that artists use overlapping to give their work a more realistic appearance. Point out how Van Gogh used vibrant colors and swirling brush strokes to convey emotion and emphasize the light in the sky and reflecting off the landscape.

Tell children that they will follow a step-by-step lesson to create their own Van Gogh-inspired pictures. Pass out the materials. Then, tape a length of blue bulletin board paper to the chalkboard and demonstrate the procedures as children follow along.

Timesaving Tip!

Set up the watercolor paint station ahead of time. Cover a table with newspaper and place the watercolors, water containers, and paintbrushes on it. You might cover all the colors in the paint trays except purple with masking tape.

Step by Step

1. To create a frame for the picture, use chalk to draw a large rectangle just inside the edges of the blue paper.

2. Draw a tall triangle-shaped tree on the left side of the paper. Add one or two smaller trees, overlapping the trees near their bases.

3. To the right of the trees, draw a curvy horizon line to represent hills.

4. For the village, draw a rectangle-shaped building in the middle of the page. Add a tall, narrow triangle-shaped steeple. Then, draw other buildings next to and around this one. Be sure to overlap some of the buildings.

5. Draw swirls, spirals, and broken lines to create the lights in the sky. Accent these lines by tracing them with white, yellow, and orange oil pastels.

6. Trace the rest of the drawing with a dark green oil pastel and color the trees, hills, and village with the pastel colors of your choice. Use yellow on windows or other any areas where you want to emphasize the glow or reflection of light.

7. Take your drawing to the watercolor paint station. Brush a purple watercolor wash over areas of the picture not filled in with oil pastels. Be sure to outline the swirls and spirals in the sky to give them more energy.

One Step More

Display the completed projects on a bulletin board covered with black paper. Title the display "Starry Night."

Language Arts Link

Write *star* on a sheet of chart paper. Ask children to say the word and listen for the *ar* sound in it. Then, have them brainstorm other words that contain this *r*-controlled vowel, such as *bar, car, chart, hard,* and *yarn.* List their responses on the chart. After reviewing the words, write each one on a star cutout. Invite pairs of children to use the star flash cards to practice reading words containing *ar*. Ask more advanced children to write a story using as many *ar* words as possible. Have them write the used *ar* words on star cutouts, border their papers with the stars, and then display the stories for others to read.

Related Reading

The Starry Night by Neil Waldman (Boyds Mill Press, 1999)

Vincent's Colors by Vincent Van Gogh; produced by the Metropolitan Museum of Art Staff (Chronicle Books, 2005)

Vincent Van Gogh (Artists in Their Time) by Jen Green (Franklin Watts, 2003)

Vincent Van Gogh: Sunflowers and Swirly Stars by Joan Holub (Grosset & Dunlap, 2001)

Spring Lion and Lamb

Use these two-sided critters as a springboard to discuss the mild and wild weather of spring.

Art Concepts

color
shape
texture

Materials

To display:
- completed project
- texture reference chart (page 199)

For each child:
- 9- by 12-inch light brown and white construction paper
- pencil
- scissors
- 4-inch square of orange and manila construction paper

To share:
- 12 tagboard body, lion head, and lamb head templates (page 181)
- glue sticks
- 1- by 3-inch strips of brown construction paper (about 12 per child)
- color markers
- 2–inch squares of black construction paper
- scraps of white and brown construction paper

Let's Begin

Discuss the phrase "In like a lion, out like a lamb." After sharing, show children the completed project. Explain that each side of the project represents a type of weather associated with spring: wild and mild. Then, have children name the colors and shapes used to make the project. Point out the curled paper-strip mane and fur lines on the lion. Flip the project over and point out the curly wool on the lamb. Explain that several techniques were used to create texture and help make each animal appear more realistic. Finally, display the texture reference chart and have children find other designs that might be used to give texture to a picture of a lion or lamb.

Tell children that they will create a two-sided lion and lamb. Pass out the materials and demonstrate the procedures as children follow along.

Timesaving Tip!

Use a paper cutter to cut the construction paper into the sizes needed for the project. You can stack and cut several sheets at a time.

Step by Step

1. For the lion, fold the 9- by 12-inch light brown paper in half vertically. Place the body template with the straight edge along the fold. Trace the template with pencil. Cut out and unfold the shape to reveal the body.

2. Trace the lion head template on the 4-inch square of orange paper. Cut out the shape and glue it onto the lion's body. For the mane, glue 1- by 3-inch strips of brown paper around the lion's head, trapping one end of each strip just under the head.

Curl mane with pencil.

Strips for mane.

3. Use a marker to draw a face, fur, and other features on the lion. You might cut out ears from scrap paper and glue them onto the lion. To curl the mane, wrap the loose end of each strip tightly around a pencil and then release it.

4. For the lamb's body, repeat Step 1 using the 9- by 12-inch white paper. Then, trace the lamb head template onto the 4-inch square of manila paper, cut out the shape, and glue it onto the lamb's body.

5. Cut out oval-shaped ears from two 2-inch squares of black paper and a cloud-shaped tuft of wool from white scrap paper (for the head). Glue the cutouts onto the lamb.

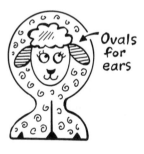

Ovals for ears

6. Use a marker to draw a face, wool, and other features on the lamb.

7. Glue the completed lion and lamb together back-to-back.

One Step More

Punch a hole in the top of the two-sided critter, add a yarn hanger, and suspend it from the ceiling or on a clothesline to display.

Language Arts Link

Have children say *lion* and *lamb*. How are the two words alike? After stating that both words begin with *L*, have children brainstorm other words that begin with the same sound. List their responses on chart paper. Then, have them write and illustrate some of the words from the list on a large cutout of a block letter *L*. Challenge more advanced children to use as many *L* words as possible to write and illustrate alliterative sentences that make sense.

Related Reading

If I Were a Lion by Sarah Weeks (Atheneum, 2004)

Our Wild World: Lions by Cherie Winner (Northwood Press, 2001)

When Spring Comes by Robert Maas (Henry Holt & Company, 1996)

Wild and Woolly by Mary Jessie Parker (Dutton Juvenile, 2005)

Fly-High Kite

Children can explore the windy weather of spring with these kites that actually fly!

Art Concepts
line
shape
pattern

Materials

To display:
- completed project

For each child:
- kite pattern (page 182)
- pencil
- fine-tip black permanent marker
- two drinking straws
- two 18-inch lengths of kite string

To share:
- regular and fluorescent crayons (one box of each for every two children)
- scissors
- tape

Let's Begin

Tell children that windy days and kite-flying are often associated with spring weather. Display the completed project and ask children to tell what a six-sided shape, such as the kite, is called. After concluding that the kite is a hexagon, point out the border around its edges. Have children identify the kinds of lines and any shapes found in the border. Can they find a pattern in the border? Explain that a pattern is formed by repeated lines, shapes, or colors. Finally, have children identify any lines and shapes used to decorate the kite inside the border.

Tell children that they will use lines and shapes to create a pattern and a picture on a kite. Pass out the materials and demonstrate the procedures as children follow along.

Timesaving Tip!
Precut all the straws to 6-inch lengths. Use a large plastic needle to thread the strings through the straws.

Step by Step

1. Use the pencil to draw a repeating pattern around the inside border of the kite shape. You might use lines, shapes, or a combination of lines and shapes.

2. Trace the repeating pattern with the fine-tip marker. Then, color the pattern, making sure to use the same color pattern around the entire border.

3. Draw a picture in the middle of the kite. Fill this space with a large drawing of one object rather than several small objects (for example, a butterfly, flower, clown, or cat). Color the picture in the colors of your choice.

4. Cut out the kite. Tape the two straws to the back of the kite as shown. Then, trim the straws to fit the kite.

5. Thread an 18-inch length of string through each straw and tie the ends together. Then, tie the ends to another length of string to use for flying the kite.

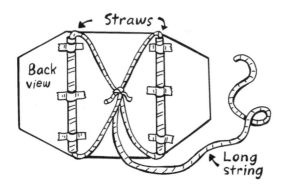

One Step More

Take children outdoors on a mildly windy day to fly their kites.

Language Arts Link

Write *kite* on the chalkboard. Say the word and ask children to tell what vowel sound they hear. Have them brainstorm other words that contain the long *i* sound, such as *flight, life, mile, nice,* and *ride.* Write their responses on the board and review the words with children. Ask volunteers to underline each long *i* word that is spelled with the CVCe pattern. Then, have children use these words to make up short rhymes about the wind and flying kites. Have more advanced children sort the words to create a word family chart and then add as many more words as possible to each word family group.

Related Reading

The Emperor and the Kite by Jane Yolen (Putnam Juvenile, 1998)

Feel the Wind by Arthur Dorros (HarperTrophy, 1990)

Gilberto and the Wind by Marie Hall Ets (Puffin, 1978)

Kite Flying by Grace Lin (Dragonfly Books, 2004)

3-D Leprechaun

Invite children to create these lively leprechauns to celebrate the traditions and symbols of St. Patrick's Day.

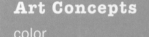

Art Concepts

color
shape
two-dimensional
three-dimensional

Materials

To display:

- pictures of leprechauns (see Related Reading for books featuring leprechaun pictures)
- completed project

For each child:

- 6- by 8-inch green crepe paper
- paper towel
- pencil
- scissors
- green construction paper: two 1½ by 6-inch strips; two 1½ by 9-inch strips; 4- by 6-inch rectangle
- two 3- by 4-inch pieces of black construction paper
- black crayon

To share:

- glue sticks
- 12 tagboard head, hand, boot and hat templates (page 183)
- 6-inch and 3-inch squares of construction paper in assorted flesh colors
- scraps of green, orange, black, and yellow construction paper
- scraps of gold and green foil wrapping paper

Let's Begin

Display the leprechaun pictures and the completed project. Discuss the symbols and traditions of St. Patrick's Day, including leprechauns, shamrocks, and the pot of gold. Ask children to examine the display items and name the most common color used for the leprechauns' clothes. What other colors are used? Next, help them find and name different shapes in the pictures and project. Point out that the body and limbs of the leprechaun project are three-dimensional because they have width, height, and depth. Then, tell children that the head, hat, and hands are two-dimensional because they are made of flat shapes—they have only width and height, but no depth.

Inform children that they will create a three-dimensional leprechaun. Pass out the materials and demonstrate the procedures as children follow along.

Timesaving Tip!

Use a paper cutter to cut the construction paper in the sizes needed for the project. You can stack and cut several sheets of paper at a time.

Step by Step

1. To make the body, fold the 6- by 8-inch green crepe paper in half horizontally. Glue two of the open edges together to form a pocket. Then, stuff a crumpled paper towel into the opening and glue the pocket shut.

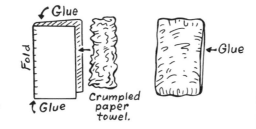

Fold
Glue
Glue
Crumpled paper towel.
Glue

2. Use pencil to trace the head template onto a 6-inch square of flesh-colored paper. Cut out the shape and glue it to the body.

3. Accordion-fold the 6-inch and 9-inch strips of green construction paper. For arms, glue the 6-inch strips to each side of the body. Glue the 9-inch strips to the bottom of the body to serve as legs.

Glue

4. Use pencil to trace the hand template onto two 3-inch squares of flesh-colored paper. Trace the boot template onto two 3- by 4-inch pieces of black construction paper. Cut out all the shapes. Glue each hand to the end of an arm and each boot to the end of a leg.

5. Choose a hat template, trace it onto the 4- by 6-inch green paper, and cut out the shape. Glue the hat onto the head.

6. Cut out hair, clothing accessories, and other items (such as a pot of gold) from scraps of construction and wrapping paper. Glue on each piece. Finally, draw the face and other details with the black crayon.

One Step More

Display the leprechauns on a bulletin board along with large shamrock cutouts labeled with information about leprechauns and St. Patrick's Day.

MATH
READING
SCIENCE
HISTORY
READING

Language Arts Link

Explain that according to legend, leprechauns hide their pot of gold at the end of a rainbow. Invite children to imagine they are leprechauns. Where in the classroom would they hide their gold? Invite one child at a time to secretly hide a cutout of a pot of gold, whisper the location of the gold to you, and then call out step-by-step directions to a small group to lead them to the treasure. Ask more advanced children to write the directions to their hidden gold.

Related Reading

It's St. Patrick's Day by Rebecca Gomez (Cartwheel, 2004)

Jack and the Leprechaun by Ivan Robertson (Random House Books for Young Readers, 2000)

Leprechauns Never Lie by Lorna Balian (Star Bright Books, 2004)

That's What Leprechauns Do by Eve Bunting (Clarion Books, 2006)

Rainbow City

Reinforce children's knowledge of rainbows and the colors of the rainbow with these multi-colored pictures.

Art Concepts

primary color
secondary color
shape

Materials

To display:
- color wheel (page 197)
- completed project

For each child:
- 12- by 18-inch white construction paper
- black crayon
- scissors
- crayons

To share:
- red, orange, yellow, green, blue, and purple construction paper shapes in assorted sizes (circles, triangles, squares, rectangles, and so on)
- glue sticks

Let's Begin

Discuss with children how a rainbow is formed and the colors of the rainbow. You might share the acronym ROY G. BIV to help them remember the sequence of colors (red, orange, yellow, green, blue, indigo, and violet). Then, show them the completed project. Can they find the colors of the rainbow in the picture? Tell children that indigo is often combined with blue and that violet is more commonly called purple. Point out that each primary color (red, yellow, and blue) in the sequence is followed by a secondary color (orange, green, and purple). Have children compare the sequence of colors in a rainbow to the order in which they are arranged on the color wheel. Then, ask them to name the shapes in the picture. Explain that this is called a rainbow city because every object in the picture is in a color found in a rainbow.

Tell children that they will create a rainbow city using paper in the colors of the rainbow. Pass out the materials and demonstrate the procedures as children follow along.

Timesaving Tip!

Use a paper cutter and die-cutter to cut out an assortment of paper shapes in the colors of the rainbow. You can stack and cut several layers of paper at a time.

Step by Step

1. Use the black crayon to draw a large rectangle just inside the edges of the white paper. This will be the border or frame for your picture. Decorate the frame with striped lines, shapes, swirls, or any other design of your choice.

2. Choose a red shape to use for a building, tree, or other object that might be seen in a city scene. You might trim the shape to round the corners, give it jagged edges, or make it interesting in some other way. Glue the shape to the left side of the picture. If desired, you might use more than one red shape to create the building or object.

3. Repeat Step 2 using orange shapes to create the next building or object. Then, repeat Step 2 again using yellow, green, blue, and purple shapes, in that order. The color sequence of your city scene should follow the sequence of the color bands in a rainbow. If space allows, start the color sequence over again until you run out of space on the paper.

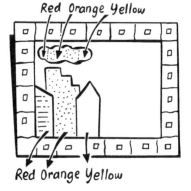

4. Use crayons to add objects to the sky, such as birds, airplanes, clouds, and so on. Color each sky object the same color as the object directly below it, even if you need to use more than one color to do this.

One Step More

Display the pictures on a bulletin board covered in black paper and titled "Rainbow City."

Language Arts Link

Write the color words *red*, *orange, yellow, green, blue, purple, black, brown,* and *white* on a sheet of chart paper. Have children read the words together. Then, point to one color word at a time. Call on a child to read the word and then find an object in the room that matches that color. After giving children practice in reading color words, have them create booklets. To do this, they write each color word on a separate sheet of paper, draw pictures in that color on the page, and staple their pages together between two covers. Challenge more advanced children to write a short poem about each color on the corresponding color page of their booklet.

Related Reading

All the Colors of the Rainbow by Allan Fowler (Children's Press, 1999)

Planting a Rainbow by Lois Ehlert (Voyager Books, 1992)

Rainbow and You by Edwin C. Krupp (HarperCollins, 2000)

Pretty Parrot

Use these colorful parrots in a discussion about ways children can help take care of the earth.

Art Concepts

color
shape
two-dimensional
three-dimensional

Materials

To display:
- completed project

For each child:
- 9- by 12-inch green construction paper
- scissors
- 4½- by 10-inch yellow construction paper
- pencil
- two 4½- by 5-inch sheets of yellow construction paper

To share:
- glue sticks
- 2- by 12-inch strips of tissue paper in bright colors (at least six per child)
- 12 tagboard beak and foot templates (page 184)
- scraps of construction paper in bright colors
- 12-inch lengths of crepe streamers in assorted colors

Let's Begin

Share Lynne Cherry's *The Great Kapok Tree: A Tale of the Amazon Rain Forest* or Kristin Joy Pratt's *A Walk in the Rainforest*. Then, discuss some of the ecological issues mentioned in the book and ways children can help take care of the earth. Afterward, show them the completed project. Point out the bright colors used for the parrot's head, beak, feathers, and tail. Have children name the shapes used to make the bird. Explain that the project is constructed from a two-dimensional sheet of paper. Flat paper only has width and height, but when it is formed into a cylinder, it takes on another dimension—depth. Conclude by telling children that the parrot is three-dimensional and has a more realistic appearance than that of a flat paper bird.

Tell children that they will create a colorful parrot. Pass out the materials and demonstrate the procedures as children follow along.

Timesaving Tip!

Use a paper cutter to cut the construction and tissue paper in the sizes needed for the project. You can stack and cut several sheets of paper at a time.

Step by Step

1. To make feathers, stack three colors of 2- by 12-inch tissue paper strips and fringe one long edge through all layers. Repeat with three more strips.

2. Glue a fringed strip along the long edge of the 9- by 12-inch green paper. Glue another strip about an inch above the first one. Continue gluing the remaining strips onto the paper in this manner.

3. For the beak, fold the 4½- by 10-inch yellow paper in half. Place the narrow end of the beak template along the fold, trace the shape in pencil, and cut it out through both layers. Unfold the shape and then fold about ½-inch of each end toward the center fold line. Glue the beak onto the middle of the green paper just above the top row of feathers as shown.

Beak

Glue

Fold

6 rows of fringe.

4. Glue the ends of the green paper together to form a tube.

Glue ends together to make tube.

5. Trace the foot template onto each 4½- by 5-inch yellow paper. Cut out the shapes and glue them to the bottom of the bird.

6. Cut out eyes from paper scraps and glue them onto the bird. For tail feathers, glue crepe paper streamers along the bottom of the bird. Then, fluff the feathers on the bird's body.

One Step More

To convert the project into a windsock, punch two holes opposite each other in the top of the parrot. Tie each end of a 24-inch length of yarn to a hole to create a hanger.

Language Arts Link

Ask children to pretend they are parrots that spread the word about taking care of the earth. What message would they want to share with others? Have them write (or dictate) their messages on a speech bubble cutout and attach it to their parrot's claws. Ask more advanced children to divide a strip of paper into several sections and then write a different message in each section.

Related Reading

The Great Kapok Tree: A Tale of the Amazon Rain Forest by Lynne Cherry (Voyager Books, 2000)

Just a Dream by Chris Van Allsburg (Houghton Mifflin, 1990)

Uno's Garden by Graeme Base (Abrams Books for Young Readers, 2006)

A Walk in the Rainforest by Kristin Joy Pratt (Dawn Publications, 1992)

Scratch-Art Spring Scene

Have children create and use these scenes to share what they know about recycling and keeping the environment clean.

Art Concepts

color
line
shape

Materials

To display:
- completed project
- color wheel (page 197)

For each child:
- 8-inch square of tagboard
- newspaper pad
- crayons
- 8-inch square of newsprint
- pencil
- 8-inch square of wax paper
- 4 paper clips
- watercolor paintbrush

For paint station:
- several containers of black tempera paint (add one tablespoon of liquid soap to each pint of paint)
- wide or chubby paintbrushes

Let's Begin

Display the completed project and color wheel. Tell children that the picture in the project is a scene to commemorate Earth Day. Then, discuss ways they can celebrate Earth Day every day, such as by recycling and picking up trash. Afterward, review the colors on the color wheel and have children find as many of these as possible in the picture. Explain that the project was made using a technique called "scratch art," in which the paper was colored with crayons and then coated with black paint. After the paint dried, a blunt-pointed object was used to scratch a drawing through the paint to expose the underlying colors. Finally, have children point out the different kinds of lines and shapes used in the drawing.

Tell children that they will create a scratch-art spring scene. Pass out the materials and demonstrate the procedures as children follow along.

Timesaving Tip!

Set up the paint station ahead of time. Cover a table with newspaper, mix the paint, and pour it into smaller containers. Just before beginning the activity, place the containers of paint and paintbrushes on the table.

Step by Step

1. Place the 8-inch tagboard square on the newspaper pad. Use crayons to completely color the square using enough pressure to color it heavily and evenly. You might color bands of color (as in a rainbow) or color areas of the tagboard in a random pattern.

2. Take the colored square to the paint station, cover it with a coat of black paint, and set it aside to dry (a few hours or overnight).

3. Use pencil to draw a simple spring scene on the 8-inch square of newsprint. You might draw a park, garden, or pond scene or another spring-related picture such as a bird nesting in a tree or a caterpillar munching on a leaf.

4. Stack the 8-inch wax paper and the painted square, in that order, behind the pencil drawing. Paper-clip the squares together and place them on the newspaper pad. Then, use pencil to trace the entire drawing, using enough pressure to make an impression of all the lines in the black-painted square.

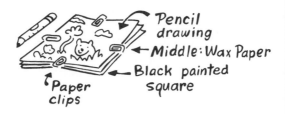

Pencil drawing

Middle: Wax Paper

Black painted square

Paper clips

5. Remove the paper clips, separate the squares, and discard the pencil drawing and wax paper. To scratch the drawing through the painted surface of the black square, use the end of the watercolor paintbrush handle to trace the lines of the impression made by the pencil. Then, scratch in other details that you'd like to add to your picture. Brush away the loose particles of paint as you work.

Scratch in details.

One Step More

Use edger scissors to create a decorative edge around a 10-inch square of colored paper. Mount the scratch art picture onto the paper to prepare it for display.

Language Arts Link

Write *scratch* and *spring* on chart paper, and underline the three-letter blend at the beginning of each word. Ask children to brainstorm other words that begin with *scr* and *spr*, such as *scream, screw, scrub, spray, spread,* and *sprout.* List their responses on chart paper. Then, have children draw a tally mark next to each word on the list as they come across it in their reading activities. If they find a new word that begins with *scr* or *spr*, have them add it to the list. At the end of the day, count to see which word appeared most often in children's reading material. Afterward, more advanced children can write and illustrate serious and silly sentences using words from the list.

Related Reading

Earth Day Hooray! by Stuart J. Murphy (HarperTrophy, 2004)

The Great Trash Bash by Loreen Leedy (Holiday House, 2000)

Recycle: A Handbook for Kids by Gail Gibbons (Little, Brown Young Readers, 1996)

Recycle That! by Fay Robinson (Children's Press, 1995)

Gadget-Print Critters

Use these interesting critters to discuss and compare the characteristics of birds, mammals, fish, and reptiles.

Art Concepts
shape
printmaking
pattern

Materials

To display:
- completed project

For each child:
- 12- by 18-inch white construction paper
- pencil
- scissors
- black marker

For printmaking station:
- white, black, brown, green, orange, yellow, red, and blue tempera paint
- eight paint trays
- printmaking gadgets such as thread spools, bristle blocks, pieces of corrugated cardboard, plastic soda bottle lids, and Styrofoam peanuts (two or three of each gadget for every paint color)
- supply of moist paper towels
- plastic gloves (optional)

Let's Begin

Display the completed project and ask children to identify the animal. Is it a mammal, bird, fish, or reptile? After sharing their responses, discuss the characteristics of the different animal groups. Then, point out the shapes on the project. Explain that they were made by dipping a gadget into paint and printing it onto the animal cutout. Tell children that many kinds of gadgets can be used for printmaking, including thread spools, bottle caps, and blocks. Then, call their attention to the repeated use of the same print on the animal. Tell them that when a shape is repeated in this way it creates a pattern.

Inform children that they will create a gadget-print animal. Pass out the materials. Then, demonstrate the procedures and have children follow along.

Timesaving Tip!

Set up a printmaking station ahead of time. Cover a large table with newspaper, add a half-inch layer of moist paper towels to each paint tray, and place the trays and printmaking gadgets on the table. Just before beginning the activity, spread a different color paint onto the towels in each tray.

Step by Step

1. Use pencil to draw a large outline of an animal on the white paper. You might draw a fish, chicken, snake, turtle, rabbit, or any animal of your choice. Be sure to make the animal as large as possible. Then, cut out the shape.

2. Take the cutout to the printmaking station. Choose a gadget and use the paint color of your choice to create gadget-prints on the cutout. You might make gadget-prints in several different colors, but be sure to use the same gadget for all the prints. You can wipe the paint off the gadget with a moist paper towel before dipping it into a different color paint. (If available, wear plastic gloves to avoid getting paint on your hands.)

3. After the prints dry, use the marker to draw a face and other details on your animal.

One Step More

Divide and label a bulletin board with the different animal groups represented by the projects. Display each gadget-print critter with its corresponding group.

Language Arts Link

Tell children that the real animals represented by their projects move about and are active in many different ways. Explain that action words are called verbs. Then, invite children to pretend to be crazy critters. Tell them that you will call out one word at a time. If the word is a verb, such as *crawl*, *hop*, *fly*, or *swim*, they will perform that action. If the word is not a verb, they will remain quiet and still. Have more advanced children choose an animal and then use as many verbs as possible to write about its daily activities. Have them underline each verb that appears in their writing.

Related Reading

About Birds: A Guide for Children by Cathryn Sill (Peachtree Publishers, 1997)

About Mammals: A Guide for Children by Cathryn Sill (Peachtree Publishers, 1997)

All Kinds of Animals by Sally Hewitt (Children's Press, 1999)

Animals Born Alive and Well by Ruth Heller (Putnam Juvenile, 1999)

3-D Pond

Invite children to explore the different kinds of plants and animals that live in a pond environment with these unique 3-D projects.

Art Concepts

shape
two-dimensional
three-dimensional

Materials

To display:

- pictures of pond life (see Related Reading for books featuring pictures of pond life)
- completed project

For each child:

- 9- by 12-inch light brown construction paper
- scissors
- 6- by 8-inch turquoise construction paper
- pencil
- thin-tip color markers

To share:

- glue sticks
- scraps of construction paper in assorted colors and shapes

Let's Begin

Show children the pictures of pond life and the completed project. Discuss the different kinds of plants and animals that live in a pond environment. Then, call children's attention to the shapes found in the living things around the pond. Have them name the shapes they see. Point out that the project is made from different sizes and shapes of paper. Inform children that a flat piece of paper is two-dimensional because it only has width and height. When the paper is shaped into a form that has depth, it becomes three-dimensional. Ask them to point out the two- and three-dimensional objects in the project.

Tell children that they will create a 3-D pond from paper. Pass out the materials and demonstrate the procedures as children follow along.

Timesaving Tip!

Create the pond basins in Step 1 ahead of time. You can stack and cut several sheets of brown paper at a time and then have volunteers help you form them into the bowl shapes.

Step by Step

1. Use scissors to round each corner of the light brown paper to give it an oval shape. Then, at each rounded corner, cut a 2-inch slit toward the center of the oval. Overlap and glue the slit edges together, as shown, to create a bowl-shaped pond basin.

2. For water, round the corners of the turquoise paper. Glue the paper to the bottom of the pond.

3. Use pencil to draw simple outlines of pond animals, such as turtles, fish, snails, and ducks, on pieces of scrap paper. Cut out each shape. Use the marker to draw details on the animals. Then, glue them onto the pond. To make an animal appear to be sitting on the water, fold the bottom of the animal (such as a duck) and glue only the folded side to the pond.

4. To make 3-D reeds or cattails, roll a rectangular piece of scrap paper into a tube and glue the end in place. Cut short slits all around the top and bottom of the tube. Then, spread the slits at one end and glue them onto the pond. For cattails, add cutouts of the stalks to the top of the slit tube.

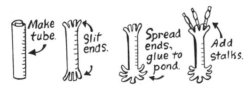

One Step More

To display, cover a table top or other flat surface with shredded green paper or cellophane grass. Then, nest the 3-D ponds into the grass.

Language Arts Link

Read Denise Fleming's *In the Small, Small Pond* or Cathryn Falwell's *Turtle Splash! Countdown at the Pond*. Afterward, ask children to name some sounds they might hear at a pond. Have them listen closely to the beginning sound of each of their responses. What letter might that sound begin with? After deciding, write the word for the sound on chart paper. When finished, invite children to write pond-related sentences or rhymes that contain one or more sounds from the chart. Have them illustrate their pages and then bind them into a class booklet. More advanced children can pretend to be a pond critter and then write a story about that critter's experiences at the pond.

Related Reading

In the Small, Small Pond by Denise Fleming (Henry Holt & Company, 1998)

Pond by Donald Silver (McGraw-Hill, 1997)

Pond Year by Kathryn Lasky (Candlewick, 1995)

Turtle Splash! Countdown at the Pond by Cathryn Falwell (Greenwillow, 2001)

Farmer Rabbit

Children can use these furry farmer friends to share their knowledge of the importance of farms and farmers.

Art Concepts

shape
pattern
texture

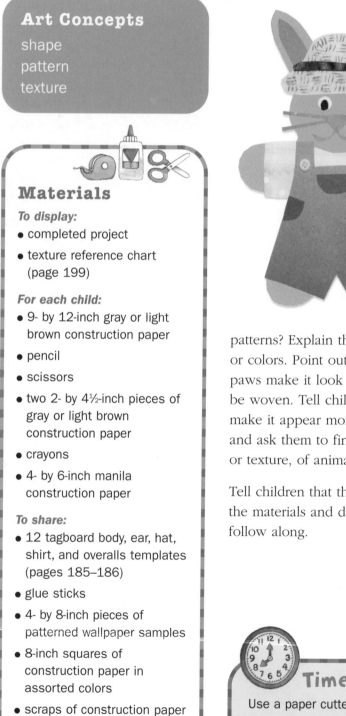

Materials

To display:
- completed project
- texture reference chart (page 199)

For each child:
- 9- by 12-inch gray or light brown construction paper
- pencil
- scissors
- two 2- by 4½-inch pieces of gray or light brown construction paper
- crayons
- 4- by 6-inch manila construction paper

To share:
- 12 tagboard body, ear, hat, shirt, and overalls templates (pages 185–186)
- glue sticks
- 4- by 8-inch pieces of patterned wallpaper samples
- 8-inch squares of construction paper in assorted colors
- scraps of construction paper in assorted colors

Let's Begin

Discuss with children the role that farmers have in the community. What do they do and why are they important? Afterward, show them the completed project. Have children name the shapes used in the project. Do they see any patterns? Explain that a pattern is formed by repeated lines, shapes, or colors. Point out how the lines on the rabbit's face, ears, and paws make it look furry and the lines on the hat make it appear to be woven. Tell children that these lines give the project texture and make it appear more realistic. Show them the texture reference chart and ask them to find designs that might resemble the appearance, or texture, of animal fur or a woven hat.

Tell children that they will create a farmer rabbit. Pass out the materials and demonstrate the procedures while children follow along.

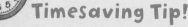

Timesaving Tip!

Use a paper cutter to cut the construction paper and wallpaper samples to the sizes needed for the project.

Step by Step

1. Fold the 8- by 12-inch paper in half lengthwise. Use pencil to trace the rabbit template onto the paper. Cut out the shape through both layers of paper. Then, unfold the shape.

2. Trace the ear template onto the two 2- by 4½-inch pieces of paper. Cut out both shapes. Then, glue each ear to the rabbit.

3. For the shirt, choose a piece from the wallpaper samples. Trace the shirt template onto the back of the sample. Cut out the shape, turn it over, and glue it onto the rabbit.

4. Choose an 8-inch square of construction paper for the overalls. Trace the template onto the paper and cut out the shape. Glue the overalls over the shirt.

5. Cut out facial features, overall pockets and buttons, and other details from scrap paper. Glue each piece onto the rabbit. Then, use crayons to draw on other details, such as fur, whiskers and paws.

6. Trace the hat template onto the 4- by 6-inch manila paper and cut it out. Use crayons to draw a weave-like pattern on the hat and decorate it with a construction-paper band or ribbon cutout. Glue the hat on the rabbit's head.

One Step More

Glue the farmer rabbit onto a 12- by 18-inch sheet of white paper. Draw a farm scene, farm tools, and machinery on the paper surrounding the rabbit.

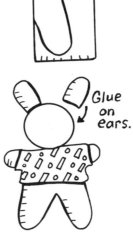

Fold

Glue on ears.

Language Arts Link

Play "The Farmer's Job" to give children practice in using descriptive language and in listening. To play, whisper to a child a job that a farmer might do, such as "feed the pigs" or "plant corn." Then, have the child describe that job to the class without using the words that label the job. When children guess correctly, invite a different child to describe another job. Have more advanced children write job descriptions on large index cards and write the job label on the back. Have them exchange cards, read the descriptions, guess the jobs, and then check to see if they guessed correctly.

Related Reading

Farmers by Alice K. Flanagan (Compass Point Books, 2002)

If It Weren't for Farmers by Allan Fowler (Children's Press, 1994)

If You Were a Farmer by Virginia Schomp (Benchmark Books, 2000)

Living on Farms by Allan Fowler (Children's Press, 2000)

Eraser-Print Pig

Have children create these adorable pigs to practice counting, patterning, and other important math skills.

Art Concepts

shape
symmetry
pattern

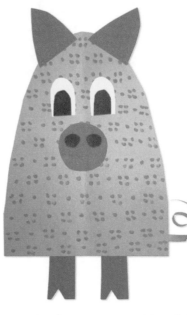

Materials

To display:
- completed project

For each child:
- 9- by 12-inch medium pink construction paper
- pencil
- scissors
- four 3-inch squares of dark pink construction paper

To share:
- glue sticks
- scraps of black, white, and pink construction paper

For printmaking stations:
- 10 red ink stamp pads
- 20 wooden pencils with erasers

Let's Begin

Show children the completed project. Ask them to name the different shapes used to make it. Tell them that the pig has symmetry because one side of the pig is a mirror image of the other side. Have children name which parts of the pig are identical on both the left and right sides (ears, eyes, nostrils, and legs). Explain that the designs on the pig are made with pencil eraser prints. Do children see any patterns on the pig? Point out how the eraser-print designs are repeated in an alternating pattern. Tell them that a pattern is one or more designs, shapes, colors, or lines that are repeated on an object.

Inform children that they will create an eraser-print pig. Pass out the materials and demonstrate the procedure as children follow along.

Timesaving Tip!

Set up two printmaking stations ahead of time. Cover each table with newspaper and then place ten stamp pads and ten pencils on each table.

Step by Step

1. Fold the 9- by 12-inch pink paper in half lengthwise. Use pencil to draw half an arch from the top of the folded side to the bottom of the open side of the paper. Cut out and unfold the shape to use for the pig's body.

2. Take the cutout to the printmaking station. Use the eraser end of a pencil to create a repeating pattern of designs on the cutout. You might make an alternating pattern of lines with the prints (such as straight and zigzag), or you might cluster prints to make circle, square, or X designs to use in the pattern. A circle design can be made with six prints, an X with five, and a square with four prints. Choose only two different kinds of lines or designs to use on the cutout, and repeat these as often as needed to cover the entire shape.

3. Draw a pig's ear shape on a 3-inch square of dark pink paper. Stack another dark pink square behind this one, and cut out the shape through both layers of paper. Glue the ears to the top of the pig cutout.

4. For the feet, repeat Step 3 using a pig's foot shape. Glue the feet to the bottom of the pig cutout.

5. Cut out a pig snout, tail, nostrils, and eyes from scrap paper. Glue each piece onto the pig. To curl the tail, wrap it tightly around a pencil and then release it.

One Step More

Display the projects on a bulletin board covered with black paper. Title the display "Piggy Patterns."

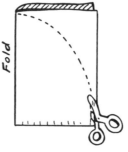

Fold

Eraser Print Designs

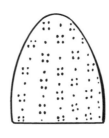

Language Arts Link

Tell children that *pig* begins with *p*. Ask them to brainstorm other words that begin with *p*, such as *pan, pet, pick, pond,* and *puppy*. List their responses on chart paper. Then, have children use words from the list to make up a class story about a pig. Instruct them to take turns adding to the story so that every child has a chance to contribute. Challenge more advanced children to write alliterative sentences with every word beginning with *p*, such as "Pink pigs pick pears." Before beginning, ask them to sort the list of *p* words by parts of speech: noun, verb, and adjective. Then, they can refer to the chart to find words to use in their sentences.

Related Reading

All Pigs Are Beautiful by Dick King-Smith (Candlewick, 2001)

The Piggy in the Puddle by Charlotte Pomerantz (Aladdin, 1989)

Pigs by Sara Swan Miller (Children's Press, 2000)

Pigs Aplenty, Pigs Galore! by David McPhail (Puffin, 1996)

Baby Chicks in a Basket

*Invite children to use these cute, spring chicks to review
the stages in the life cycle of a chicken.*

Art Concepts

shape
two-dimensional
three-dimensional
texture

Materials

To display:
- completed project

For each child:
- three 3- by 8-inch sheets of yellow crepe paper
- glue stick
- scissors
- plastic strawberry basket

To share:
- white tissue paper or newsprint
- scraps of yellow, orange, black, and white construction paper
- shredded green paper or cellophane grass

Let's Begin

Show children the completed project. Then, discuss the stages of a chicken's life cycle. Which stage do the chicks in the project represent? Afterward, have children name the shapes that are used in the project. Explain that the chicks were made from flat pieces of crepe paper which were formed into pockets and stuffed. Flat paper is a shape that has only two-dimensions—width and height, but when it is formed in a way so that it has a front, back, and sides, the paper becomes three-dimensional—it has width, height, and depth. Conclude by pointing out how the texture of the crepe paper gives the chicks a more realistic appearance.

Tell children that they will make crepe-paper chicks to display in a basket. Pass out the materials. Then, demonstrate the procedures while children follow along.

Timesaving Tip!

Rather than cutting out scrap-paper eyes for their chicks, have children use wiggle eyes.

Fold
Glue long edges.

Stuff and glue. Glue

Step by Step

1. To make the chicks, fold each piece of yellow crepe paper in half horizontally. Glue the long edges together, leaving the short edges open to form a pocket. Set the pockets aside until the glue is thoroughly dry (about an hour).

2. Carefully turn each pocket inside out. Then, stuff each one with torn pieces of tissue paper or newsprint. Glue together the opening of each pocket.

3. Cut out eyes, beaks, wings, and other details from scrap paper. Glue each piece onto the chicks.

4. Line the bottom of the strawberry basket with a layer of shredded green paper or cellophane grass. Place the chicks in the basket.

One Step More

Draw a large chicken on 9- by 12-inch light brown construction paper. Color and cut out the chicken and attach it to the back of the basket of chicks to create a happy hen and her baby chicks.

Language Arts Link

Write *chicken* and *scratch* on chart paper. Underline *ch* in each word and explain that this digraph has the same sound whether at the beginning or end of a word. Then, ask children to brainstorm other words that begin and end with *ch*, such as *chat*, *chop*, *hatch*, and *rich*. Then, invite them to play "Chicken Scratch." Explain that if you call out a word that begins with *ch*, children will do a chicken walk. If the word ends in *ch*, they will scratch around like chickens. If there is no *ch* in the word, they will sit as if on a nest. More advanced children can list the *ch* words they come across in their reading materials, grouping them according to whether the *ch* is at the beginning or end of the words.

Related Reading

Chickens Aren't the Only Ones by Ruth Heller (Putnam Juvenile, 1999)

From Egg to Chicken by Robin Nelson (Lerner Publications, 2003)

Hedgie's Surprise by Jan Brett (Putnam Juvenile, 2000)

Where Do Chicks Come From? by Amy E. Sklansky (HarperTrophy, 2005)

Spring Banner

How does your garden grow? Children can use these beautiful banners to share what they know about plant needs and growth.

Art Concepts

line
shape
overlap
crayon resist

Let's Begin

Discuss with children what plants need to grow and how they grow (from seed to flower). Then, display the completed project. Have children identify the different kinds of lines and shapes on the banner. Point out how some of the plants partially cover, or overlap, others. Explain that artists use overlapping to make a picture look more realistic. Tell children that the banner was created using a technique called "crayon resist," in which waxy oil pastels were used to color the picture and then a wash of water-thinned paint was painted over the picture. The wax in the colored part of the picture repelled the paint, but the uncolored parts of the paper absorbed it to create an interesting color effect.

Tell children that they will create a crayon-resist spring banner. Pass out the materials and demonstrate the procedures as children follow along.

Materials

To display:
- completed project

For each child:
- 12- by 18-inch white construction paper
- pencil
- scissors
- black marker
- oil pastels

For paint stations:
- 16 easel paintbrushes
- two containers each of magenta, orange, yellow, and blue tempera paint (one part paint mixed with two parts water)

Timesaving Tip!

Set up the paint stations ahead of time. Cover two tables with newspaper. Then, mix the paints and pour them into smaller containers. Just before beginning the activity, place two colors of paint on each table. Add four paintbrushes for every paint color.

Step by Step

1. Place the paper vertically on the table. Use pencil to draw a curvy, zigzag, castle-top, or other kind of line along the bottom edge of the paper. Cut along the line to create a decorative bottom edge for the banner.

2. Use pencil to draw a zigzag grass line about two inches above the bottom edge. Then, draw flowers in different heights from the grass line toward the top of the page. Be sure to overlap the leaves or blooms of some of the flowers. You might draw all the same kind of flowers or different flowers. To add interest, add a few garden critters, such as butterflies or beetles.

3. Trace the drawing with the black marker. Then, color the picture with oil pastels, applying enough pressure to color it heavily and evenly. Start at the top of the picture and color toward the bottom to avoid smearing the colored areas.

4. Take the drawing to the paint stations. Paint the left third of the drawing with a wash of paint in the color of your choice. Then, choose another color to paint the center of your picture, and a third color to paint the right side. Try not to mix the colors on your picture. Then, set the picture aside to dry.

One Step More

To make a hanger, back the top of the banner with a 1- by 12-inch strip of cardboard. Punch a hole in each top corner and then tie a 24-inch length of yarn to the holes.

Language Arts Link

Have children tell about what a plant needs to grow. Then, write *grow* on the chalkboard. Tell them that this word begins with the blend *gr*. Have them brainstorm other *gr* words as you write them on the board (such as *green, grass, great,* and *gray*). Have children use a ruler to draw 12 sections on a 3- by 12-inch inch strip of paper. Explain that each time they come across a word that begins with *gr*, they will write it on a line on the strip. When they fill in all the sections, they will add a flower and leaves to the strip to create a full-grown flower. Ask more advanced children to write about how plants grow. Challenge them to use as many *gr* words as possible.

Related Reading

From Seed to Plant by Allan Fowler (Children's Press, 2001)

Jack's Garden by Henry Cole (HarperTrophy, 1997)

The Reason for a Flower by Ruth Heller (Putnam Juvenile, 1999)

The Tiny Seed by Eric Carle (Aladdin, 2001)

3-D Butterfly

Encourage children to use these special critters to share their knowledge of the life cycle of a butterfly.

Art Concepts

color
symmetry
two-dimensional
three-dimensional

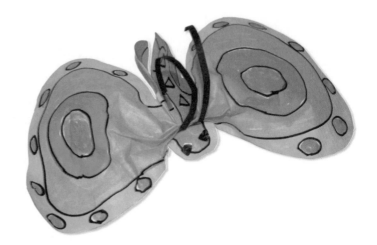

Materials

To display:
- completed project

For each child:
- 9- by 12-inch white bulletin board paper
- pencil
- scissors
- color markers

To share:
- 12 tagboard butterfly templates (page 187)
- staplers
- scraps of construction paper in assorted colors

Let's Begin

Show children the completed project. Then, discuss the stages of a butterfly's life cycle. Which stage does the project represent? Ask children to name the colors on the butterfly. Point out that a butterfly has symmetry because the colors and designs on its right side is the mirror image of its left side. Then, explain that the butterfly project was made from a flat piece of paper. Flat paper has only two-dimensions—width and height—but when it is folded in a way so that it has a front, back, and sides, the paper becomes three-dimensional—it has width, height, and depth. Finally, gently toss the butterfly into the air to show children how it can fly.

Tell children that they will create a symmetrical 3-D butterfly from paper. Pass out the materials. Then, demonstrate the procedures while children follow along.

Timesaving Tip!

Use a paper cutter to cut the white bulletin board paper into 9- by 12-inch sheets. You can stack and cut several sheets at a time.

Step by Step

1. Fold the 9- by -12-inch white paper in half lengthwise. Place the butterfly template on the fold. Trace the shape with pencil, cut it out, and unfold it to reveal a butterfly shape.

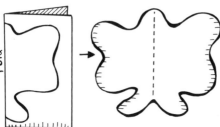

2. Use colored markers to create a design on the left side of the butterfly. Then, create a mirror image of that design on the right side.

3. Starting at the base of the head and folding toward the tail, accordion-fold the butterfly using ¾-inch folds. When finished, carefully staple the folds together.

Accordion-fold and staple.

4. Cut out eyes and antennae strips from scraps of paper. Glue the pieces onto the butterfly. To curl the antennae, wrap each one tightly around a pencil and then release it.

One Step More

To display, attach a string to the butterfly and suspend it overhead, or hang it on a bulletin board.

Language Arts Link

Explain to children that *butterfly* is a compound word. Write the two words that make up this word on the chalkboard. Then, challenge children to brainstorm other compound words. Write their responses on the board. Afterward, give children three butterfly cutouts each. Have them write the first part of a compound word on the left wing and the second part on the right wing. Then, place the cutouts in the literacy center. To use, invite children to read the individual words on each butterfly's wings and then write the compound word that the two words make when put together. Challenge more advanced children to generate lists of compound words that contain particular words, such as *house* and *sun*.

Related Reading

From Caterpillar to Butterfly by Deborah Heiligman (HarperTrophy, 1996)

The Very Hungry Caterpillar by Eric Carle (Philomel, 1981)

Waiting for Wings by Lois Ehlert (Harcourt Children's Books, 2001)

Where Butterflies Grow by Joanne Ryder (Dutton Juvenile, 1989)

Pet Yarn Paintings

Use these special pet pictures as a springboard to discuss pets and pet care.

Art Concepts

shape

texture

Materials

To display:

● completed project

For each child:

● pencil

● fat-tip permanent marker

● craft stick

● scissors

● two wiggle eyes

To share:

● 9-inch squares of colored poster board

● 5- and 6-inch round plastic lids

● oil pastels (one box for every two children)

● 12- to 24-inch lengths of thick yarn in white, brown, black, gray, yellow, green, rust, and light green

● white liquid glue

Let's Begin

Invite children to tell the class about their pets. Discuss some of the many different animals that might be kept as pets, as well as pet needs, and ways to care for them. Afterward, show children the completed project. Ask them to identify the animal and name some shapes used to create it. Explain that a technique called "yarn painting" was used to make the project. In this technique, yarn is used to fill in shapes and details to create a picture. The yarn gives the picture texture and helps it appear more realistic.

Tell children that they will create a yarn painting of their pet (or a pet they might like to have). Pass out the materials and demonstrate the procedures as children follow along.

TimeSaving Tip!

To help keep the yarn neat and organized, tie lengths of same-colored yarn together in bundles. Then, children can pull one strand of yarn at a time from a bundle as needed.

Step by Step

1. Select a poster board square in the color of your choice. To make the animal's head, use pencil to trace a 5- or 6-inch lid onto the center of the square.

2. Decide what kind of pet you want to make for your yarn painting. Then, pencil in a simple scene around the animal. Trace the lines of the scene with the black marker. Then, color the scene with oil pastels.

3. Choose the yarn color for your animal, then glue a tight spiral of yarn onto the middle of the circle. When you reach the end of that length of yarn, continue the spiral by adding another length. Add one length of yarn after another until the entire circle is covered. As you work, use small amounts of glue at a time, and press the yarn tightly into place with the craft stick.

4. Following the same technique described in Step 3, use the yarn color of your choice to create features, such as eyes and a nose, for the animal. Glue the spirals of yarn directly on top of the yarn circle. If desired, glue wiggle eyes to the center of the yarn eyes. Trim and glue on a strand of yarn to make the mouth.

5. If your animal has ears, add these in the same manner as in Step 3, working the yarn spiral in the appropriate shape for the ears (such as circles or triangles).

One Step More

To create an interesting border, display the yarn paintings around a bulletin board, door frame, or across the top of a wall.

Language Arts Link

Tell children that two common pets are cats and dogs. Write *cat* and *dog* on chart paper, and have children say the words aloud. Explain that each of these words belongs to a word family. Underline the ending of each word to show children what word family it belongs to. Then, ask them to call out words that belong to the same word families. Write each of their responses under the corresponding word. Afterward, have them create pet-related rhymes using words from the two word-family lists. Ask more advanced children to make up longer rhymes or create songs to the tune of common childhood songs.

Related Reading

Any Kind of Dog by Lynn Reiser (HarperTrophy, 1994)

The Best Thing About a Puppy by Jody Hindley (Candlewick, 1998)

Pet Show! by Ezra Jack Keats (Viking Juvenile, 2001)

Pets! by Melrose Cooper (Henry Holt & Company, 1998)

Fringed-Paper Piñata

Invite children to use these paper piñatas to share what they know about Cinco de Mayo.

Art Concepts

two-dimensional
three-dimensional
texture

Materials

To display:

- animal-shaped piñata, or picture of one (see Related Reading for books featuring piñata pictures)
- completed project
- texture reference chart (page 199)

For each child:

- pencil
- fine-tip black permanent marker
- scissors

To share:

- 12- by 18-inch construction paper in assorted colors
- oil pastels (one box for every two children)
- 1½– by 12-inch crepe paper strips in assorted colors
- glue sticks

Let's Begin

Tell children that Cinco de Mayo (Spanish for the fifth of May) is the day Mexico celebrates its victory at the Battle of Puebla. Animal-shaped piñatas—decorated containers filled with candy—are often used in these celebrations. Explain that a real piñata is three-dimensional because it has width, height, and depth. Then, show children the piñata pictures and completed project. Point out that these are two-dimensional since they have only width and height, but no depth. Discuss how the piñata project appears to have texture. Tell them that the furry-looking designs and fringed paper make the animal piñata look more realistic. Then, have children examine the texture reference chart to find designs that give the appearance of animal fur.

Inform children that they will create a fringed-paper piñata. Pass out the materials. Then, demonstrate the procedures as children follow along.

Timesaving Tip!

Use a paper cutter to cut the crepe paper strips for the project. You can stack and cut several sheets at a time.

Step by Step

1. Decide on an animal to draw for the piñata. Choose an animal with a fur covering, such as a bear, cat, or dog. Then, select a 12- by 18-inch sheet of construction paper in the color of your choice. Position it vertically or horizontally on the table, depending on the animal you plan to draw. Then, use pencil to draw a large oval body in the middle of the paper.

2. Add a head, legs, tail, and other details to the animal, but leave the oval body blank. Trace the pencil drawing with the black marker, then use the marker to draw a furry-looking texture on all parts of the animal except the oval body.

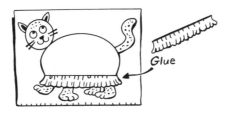

3. Use oil pastels to color all parts of the animal except the body.

4. Choose two colors of crepe paper strips to use for the body fur. Stack three or four strips together and fringe one long edge through all layers. Repeat with another stack of paper strips. The number of strips that you'll need will depend on the height of the animal's body.

5. Glue a fringed strip across the bottom part of the animal's body. Trim the strip to fit. Then, glue a strip in the other color about an inch above the first one. Continue gluing the strips onto the body about one inch above each other, making sure to alternate the colors as you go along.

Glue

One Step More

Cut loosely around the piñata. Then, punch one or two holes in the top of the piñata, add a yarn hanger, and suspend it from the ceiling or on a clothesline to display.

Related Reading

Cinco de Mayo by Mary Dodson Wade (Children's Press, 2003)

Look What Came From Mexico by Miles Harvey (Franklin Watts, 1999)

Magda's Piñata Magic by Becky Chavarria-Chairez (Arte Publico Press, 2001)

The Piñata Maker by George Ancona (Harcourt, 1994)

Geometric Birdhouse

Build up children's geometry skills when they create their own unique birdhouse from a variety of shapes.

Art Concepts

shape
color
texture

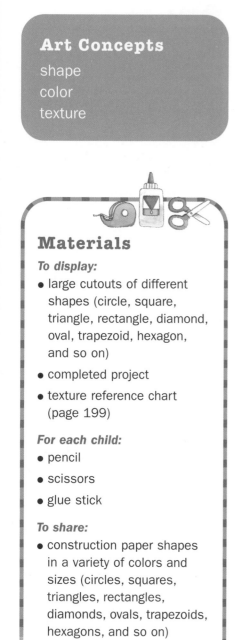

Materials

To display:

- large cutouts of different shapes (circle, square, triangle, rectangle, diamond, oval, trapezoid, hexagon, and so on)
- completed project
- texture reference chart (page 199)

For each child:

- pencil
- scissors
- glue stick

To share:

- construction paper shapes in a variety of colors and sizes (circles, squares, triangles, rectangles, diamonds, ovals, trapezoids, hexagons, and so on)
- crayons (or oil pastels)
- scraps of construction paper in assorted colors and black
- 2- and 3-inch lengths of raffia
- craft sticks

Let's Begin

Show children the shape cutouts. Encourage them to identify each shape and compare it to the other shapes. Then, show them the completed project. What shapes were used to create the birdhouse? What colors were used for the project? Talk about how the designs drawn on the siding and roof give the birdhouse a more realistic appearance. Have children refer to the texture reference chart to find designs that resemble the appearance, or texture, of materials that might be used to make a birdhouse.

Tell children that they will design a birdhouse from different geometric shapes. Pass out the materials and demonstrate the procedures as children follow along.

Timesaving Tip!

Use a die-cutter and paper cutter to cut out the construction paper shapes in a variety of sizes and colors. You can stack and cut several sheets of paper at a time.

Step by Step

1. For the base of the birdhouse, select a large shape in the color of your choice. Then, refer to the texture reference chart to find a design that most resembles the material you want the birdhouse to be "made of," such as wood, stone, straw, or brick. (Or create your own design and practice drawing it on scrap paper.) Use pencil to draw the textured design on the shape, then trace the lines with a crayon.

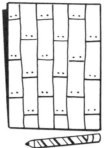

2. Select a shape in the color of your choice to use as the roof. Make sure the shape is as wide as or wider than the base. If needed, trim the shape so that it is proportionate to the base. For a rounded roof, you can use part of a circle or oval that has been cut in two. Use pencil to draw shingles, straw, or another kind of textured design on the roof. Trace the design with crayon. Glue the roof onto the base.

Make a roof.

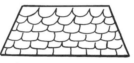

3. Cut a door from scrap paper. The door might be a circle, square, rectangle, or any other shape. Cut out windows and any other details for the birdhouse from scrap paper. Glue all the pieces onto the birdhouse.

4. Glue one end of a craft stick near the door so that it appears to be a perch extending from the door. Add raffia along the bottom edge (or rim) of the door to give the appearance of a nest inside the birdhouse.

One Step More

Attach the birdhouse to an upside-down foam or paper cup (the size will depend on the size of the birdhouse). To display, set the birdhouse on a flat surface, such as a bookshelf or window ledge.

Language Arts Link

Review a list of directional and positional words with children. Use the birdhouses to reinforce the concepts these words represent. First, have children make simple bird stick puppets. Then, have them set their birdhouses on the edge of a table. To use, have children move their puppets according to your directions, such as "fly the bird around the house," "sit the bird on top of the house," or "land the bird on the left side of the house." Each time, point out the directional or positional word used in the directions. Ask more advanced children to write an imaginary story about their bird's adventure. Have them underline words in their story that describe a position or direction.

Related Reading

Albert by Donna Jo Napoli (Silver Whistle, 2001)

The Best Nest by P. D. Eastman (Random House Books for Young Readers, 1968)

Birds in Your Backyard by Barbara Herkert (Dawn Publications, 2001)

In the Nest by Anna Milbourne (Usborne Books, 2005)

Cool Clay Pendants

Have children create these colorful pendants to practice their patterning skills.

Art Concepts
color
pattern
texture

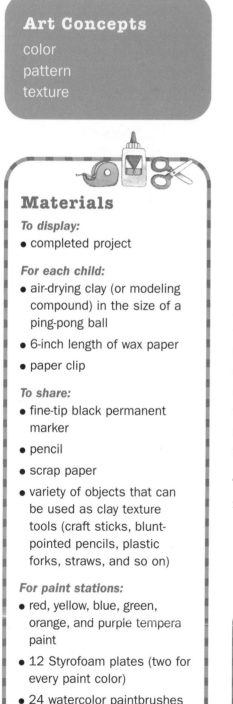

Materials

To display:
- completed project

For each child:
- air-drying clay (or modeling compound) in the size of a ping-pong ball
- 6-inch length of wax paper
- paper clip

To share:
- fine-tip black permanent marker
- pencil
- scrap paper
- variety of objects that can be used as clay texture tools (craft sticks, blunt-pointed pencils, plastic forks, straws, and so on)

For paint stations:
- red, yellow, blue, green, orange, and purple tempera paint
- 12 Styrofoam plates (two for every paint color)
- 24 watercolor paintbrushes (four for every paint color)

Let's Begin

Show children the completed project. Ask them to name the colors used in the pendant. Do they see a pattern on the project? Have them point out and describe the pattern. Explain that a pattern is created when a line, shape, or color is repeated in a design. Then, call their attention to the lines etched into the pendant. Tell them that these lines create visual and tactile texture. Visual texture can be seen, while tactile texture can actually be felt. Invite children to rub their fingers over the surface of the pendant to feel the texture.

Tell children that they will create a clay pendant. Then, pass out the materials and demonstrate the procedures as children follow along.

Timesaving Tip!

Set up the paint stations ahead of time. Cover two large tables with newspaper, and pour a shallow layer of each paint color into two Styrofoam plates. Place three colors of paint on each table. Add four paintbrushes for every paint color.

Step by Step

1. Use a marker to write your name on a corner of the wax paper. Then, press the clay onto the wax paper, forming it into a cookie-sized patty about ½-inch thick.

Paper Clip
Wax Paper
Clay Patty

2. Push one end of the paper clip into the patty, as shown.

3. Decide what kind of design you want to create on the patty. (You can use pencil and scrap paper to plan and practice drawing the design first). You might create a repeating pattern to cover the entire surface of the patty. Or you might decide to create a patterned border that encloses a larger design, such as a butterfly. When ready, etch the design into the patty using the most appropriate tool or tools to create the pattern and texture you desire.

4. Set the patty aside to dry, keeping it on the wax paper. Drying time might take several days to a week, depending on the thickness of the patty, humidity, and room temperature.

5. Take the pendant, on the wax paper, to the paint stations. Use the colors of your choice to paint the design on the pendant. Be sure to use a pattern of colors to paint the pendant. Set the pendant aside to dry. Then, use a permanent marker to write your name on the back.

One Step More

Coat children's pendants with a clear acrylic sealer. Then, have children add a yarn hanger. They might present their pendant to a parent, friend, or other special person as a gift.

Language Arts Link

Tell children that *clay* begins with the blend *cl*. Ask them to brainstorm other words that begin with *cl*, such as *clap*, *clean*, *climb*, *clock*, and *clump*. List their responses on chart paper. Then, have children use words from the list to make up a class story. Instruct them to take turns adding to the story so that every child has a chance to contribute. Later, you might challenge more advanced children to write the words from the list in alphabetical order.

Related Reading

Busy Bugs: A Book About Patterns by Jayne Harvey (Grosset & Dunlap, 2003)

Lots and Lots of Zebra Stripes: Patterns in Nature by Stephen R. Swinburne (Boyds Mills Press, 2002)

Pattern Fish by Trudy Harris (Millbrook Press, 2000)

Shapes, Shapes, Shapes by Tana Hoban (HarperTrophy, 1996)

Designer Sneakers

Reinforce patterns, shapes, counting, and other important math concepts when children design these 3-D sneakers.

Art Concepts

pattern
two-dimensional
three-dimensional

Materials

To display:
- completed project

For each child:
- 9- by 12-inch white construction paper
- 4- by 7-inch white construction paper
- scissors
- pencil
- fine-tip black marker
- color markers
- 20-inch length of yarn

To share:
- 12 tagboard sneaker and tongue templates (page 188)
- glue sticks
- three or four hole punches

Let's Begin

Show children the completed project. Ask them to examine it and then point out and describe any patterns that they find. What kind of shapes are used on the sneaker? After discussing, tell children that the sneaker was made from a flat piece of paper. Explain that flat paper has two dimensions—width and height—so it is called two-dimensional. When paper is folded or formed into an object that has width, height, and depth, it becomes a three-dimensional form.

Tell children that they will decorate a two-dimensional shape and then form it into a 3-D sneaker. Pass out the materials and demonstrate the procedures as children follow along.

Timesaving Tip!

Use a paper cutter to cut the 4- by 7-inch white paper for the sneaker tongue. You can stack and cut several sheets of paper at a time.

Step by Step

1. Fold the 9- by 12-inch white paper in half vertically. Use pencil to trace the sneaker template onto the paper with the short straight edge along the fold. Cut out and unfold the shape. Then, trace the tongue onto the 4- by 9-inch white paper and cut it out.

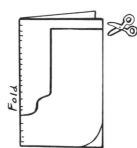

2. Use pencil to draw a line about ½-inch from the long curved edge of the sneaker cutout. Draw a repeating pattern between the line and edge. This will be the bottom edge of the sneaker. Draw shapes or designs of your choice on the remaining area of the sneaker cutout and on the wide part of the tongue cutout.

3. Use the black marker to trace the penciled drawings on the cutouts. Then, color the pattern and designs with crayons.

4. At each outer curve of the sneaker cutout, cut a 2-inch slit toward the center of the cutout. Overlap and glue the slit edges together, as shown. Then, glue the loose edges together to create a three-dimensional shoe shape.

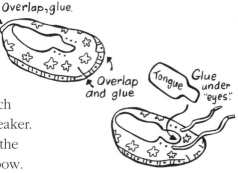

5. To make eyes for the shoelaces, use a hole punch to punch three holes along each short side of the top of the sneaker. Lace a length of yarn through the holes and tie the ends into a bow.

6. Glue the narrow end of the tongue to the sneaker just under the first set of eyes. Then, pull the tongue up through the sneaker.

One Step More

Create a pair of sneakers by making another sneaker identical to the first one.

Language Arts Link

Say *sneaker* and *feet*. Ask children to tell what long vowel sound they hear in both words. Then, write *feet* on the chalkboard. Explain that this long-vowel word follows the CVVC pattern. Have children brainstorm other one-syllable words that contain the long *e* sound, such as *bean, meet,* and *week.* Write their responses on the board. Invite volunteers to underline each word that follows the CVVC pattern. Afterward, have children use words from the list to make up short rhymes about feet. Ask more advanced children to write a creative story about feet. They can write the story on pages in the shape of foot cutouts and then bind the pages into a booklet.

Related Reading

Centipede's One Hundred Shoes by Tony Ross (Henry Holt & Company, 2003)

A Pair of Red Sneakers by Lisa Lawston (Orchard Books, 1998)

Sam Bennett's New Shoes by Jennifer Thermes (Carolrhoda Books, 2006)

In the Style of Henri Matisse: Vegetable Collage

These brightly colored collages make great discussion starters about planting and caring for a vegetable garden.

Art Concepts
shape
contrasting colors
collage

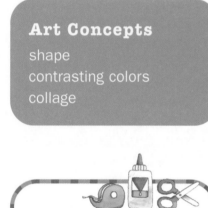

Materials

To display:
- *Les Vegetaux* by Henri Matisse (page 205)
- a variety of vegetables, real or in pictures (see Related Reading for books featuring vegetable pictures)
- completed project

For each child:
- 8- by 18-inch light gray construction paper
- pencil
- scissors

To share:
- 4-inch squares of orange and red construction paper
- 4- by 5-inch and 4- by 6-inch rectangles of orange and red construction paper
- large and small scraps of white, green, yellow, blue, and purple construction paper
- glue sticks

Let's Begin

Tell children that the French artist Henri Matisse is well-known for his brightly colored collages. Explain that a collage is created when various materials, such as paper, are glued onto the surface of the same or different kind of material. Then, have them examine *Les Vegetaux*. Ask them to name the colors used in the collage. What do the different shapes resemble? Point out how Matisse used simple background shapes and cutouts in contrasting colors. Tell children that when dark and light colors are put together, they are called contrasting colors. Afterward, show children the completed project along with the vegetables or vegetable pictures. Have them compare the shapes and colors of the vegetables on the project to the real or pictured vegetables.

Tell children that they will create a Matisse-inspired vegetable collage. Pass out the materials and demonstrate the procedure as children follow along.

Timesaving Tip!
Use a paper cutter to cut the construction paper into the sizes needed for the project. You can stack and cut several sheets of paper at a time.

Step by Step

1. Place the light gray paper vertically on the table. Position several orange and red squares and rectangles on the paper. Overlap some of the shapes and leave space between others so that some areas of the gray paper remain uncovered. When the shapes are positioned as desired, glue them down to create a three-color background for the collage.

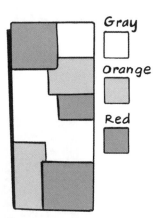

Gray

Orange

Red

2. Use pencil to draw simple vegetable outlines on several pieces of scrap paper. Use the color of your choice for each vegetable, whether it is the actual color of the real vegetable or not. You might examine the real or pictured vegetables and *Les Vegetaux* for inspiration on shapes to draw. When finished, cut out the shapes.

3. Place the vegetable cutouts on the background. Be sure to position each one against a contrasting color. You might leave a big space between some of the cutouts while placing others close together or even overlapping them. When the cutouts are positioned as desired, glue them onto the background.

One Step More

Mount the collages on 10- by 20-inch sheets of black construction paper. Display them on a bulletin board.

Language Arts Link

Tell children that *vegetable* has four syllables. Write the word on chart paper. Then, ask them to name as many vegetables as possible, such as *asparagus, lettuce, potato, squash,* and *zucchini*. Write each of their responses on the chart and have them decide how many syllables are in the word. Afterward, have children pick four vegetables from the list, each with a different syllable count. Ask them to write the word for each vegetable and then draw that vegetable as many times as there are syllables in its name. Challenge more advanced children to create a chart to sort the words on the list by syllable count.

Related Reading

Growing Vegetable Soup by Lois Ehlert (Voyager Books, 1990)

Henri Matisse: Drawing with Scissors by Jane O'Connor (Grosset & Dunlap, 2002)

Tops & Bottoms by Janet Stevens (Harcourt Children's Books, 1995)

The Ugly Vegetables by Grace Lin (Charlesbridge Publishing, 2001)

Awesome Autograph Book

Invite children to use these personalized books to collect signatures, verses, and other memorable messages from their friends.

Art Concepts

shape
pattern

Materials

To display:
- completed project

For each child:
- pencil
- color markers
- two 6- by 9-inch sheets of colored poster board
- six 5½- by 8½-inch sheets of white paper
- 12-inch length of yarn

To share:
- 4- by 6-inch construction paper in light colors
- glue sticks
- six hole punches

For printing stations:
- 24 stamps in assorted shapes (geometric shapes, animal shapes, letters, numbers, and so on)
- 12 ink pads in assorted colors

Let's Begin

Write "Autograph Book" on the chalkboard. Help children read the words. Then, talk about what an autograph book is. Afterward, show them the completed project. Point out the decorative lettering in the title. Have children name the shapes and colors used in the project. (Make sure they examine the front and back covers.) Do they see a pattern on the covers? Explain that a pattern is created when a line, shape, or design is repeated.

Tell children that they will create an autograph book that their friends can sign. Pass out the materials and demonstrate the procedures as children follow along.

Timesaving Tip!

Set up the printing stations ahead of time. Cover two tables with newspaper. Place six ink pads and nine stamps on each table.

Step by Step

1. To make the cover title, choose a 4- by 6-inch piece of paper in the color of your choice. Use pencil to write "Autograph Book" on the paper using decorative lettering, such as block, bubble, or cursive letters. Add a personal symbol or design, if desired. Trace and color in the penciled lines with markers.

2. For the front cover, glue the title paper onto the center of a 6- by 9-inch poster board. Then, stack the other poster board—the back cover—behind the front cover. Punch two holes along the left edge of the poster boards through both layers.

3. Take the covers to the printing stations. Use the stamps and ink pads to print a pattern of shapes onto both covers.

4. For the book pages, stack three 5½- by 8½-inch sheets of white paper behind the front cover, lining the paper and cover up at the left edges. Using the holes in the cover as a guide, punch holes through all the pages. Repeat for the remaining three sheets of white paper.

5. Stack the pages between the two covers. Make sure all the holes line up along the left edge. To bind the covers and pages together, string a length of yarn through the holes and tie the ends together.

One Step More

Punch a hole in the middle of the right edge of both covers. Tie a 6-inch length of yarn to each hole. Then, tie the loose ends of the yarn together in a bow to tie the book closed.

Language Arts Link

Write *awesome* and *autograph* on chart paper. Have children say the words and tell what sound is the same in both of them (*aw* and *au*). Then, help them come up with other words that contain these letter pairs, such as *caught, crawl, saw,* and *taught*. Write their responses on the chart. Afterward, ask small groups to write *au* and *aw* on paper. Set a timer and have the groups search printed materials around the room to find words spelled with *aw* and *au*. Have them write their findings on their paper. When time is up, invite the groups to share their words. Have more advanced children write their words on index cards and then use them as flash cards to practice recognizing and reading the words.

Related Reading

Chrysanthemum by Kevin Henkes (HarperTrophy, 1996)

Eleanor, Ellatony, Ellencake, and Me by Cathy Rubin (Gingham Dog Press, 2003)

My Name Is Yoon by Helen Recorvits (Farrar, Straus and Giroux, 2003)

Sunny 3-D Sunflowers

Use these big, bright sunflowers to teach children about the life cycle of a plant.

Art Concepts
shape
pattern
texture
three-dimensional

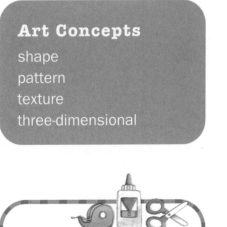

Materials

To display:
- pictures of sunflowers (see Related Reading for books featuring sunflower pictures)
- completed project
- texture reference chart (page 199)

For each child:
- 12-inch square of yellow construction paper
- pencil
- color markers, including black
- scissors
- 2- by 18-inch strip of green poster board
- three 6-inch squares of green construction paper

To share:
- 12 tagboard sunflower templates (page 189)
- twelve 3½-inch tagboard circle templates
- glue sticks

Let's Begin

Show children the sunflower pictures and completed project. Invite them to share what they know about the life cycle of a sunflower. Then, have them name the shapes they see in the pictured flowers and the project. Call their attention to the center of the sunflowers. Do they see a pattern? After sharing, explain that a pattern is formed by repeated lines, shapes, or colors. In the project, this pattern gives the flower a textured look so that it has a more realistic appearance. Have children examine the texture reference chart to find other designs that might be used to give texture to the flower. Finally, point out how the project has width, height, and depth, which make it a three-dimensional sunflower.

Tell children that they will create a three-dimensional sunflower. Pass out the materials and demonstrate the procedures as children follow along.

Timesaving Tip!
Use a paper cutter to cut the poster board and construction paper in the sizes needed for the project.

Step by Step

1. Fold the 12-inch square of yellow paper in half. Place the sunflower template along the fold and trace it onto the paper with pencil. Cut out and unfold the shape to reveal a large sunflower.

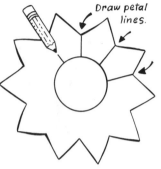

Draw petal lines.

2. Use pencil to trace a circle template on the center of the flower. To define the petals, draw a line from the circle to each V-shape on the flower, as shown. Trace the petal lines with the black marker. If desired, color every other petal orange.

3. Use pencil to draw a pattern inside the circle to represent the center of a sunflower. You might draw sunflower seeds, dots, wavy lines, or a checkerboard design (or refer to the texture reference chart for ideas). Trace the pattern with the black marker, then color it with the marker colors of your choice.

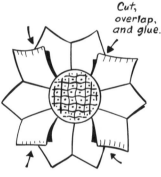

Cut, overlap, and glue.

4. Cut a slit along one of the petal lines to the circle. Skip a petal line and cut along the next one. Then, cut along the two petal lines directly opposite these two lines. Overlap and glue together the edges of each slit to form a 3-D flower, as shown.

5. For the stem, glue the flower to one end of the green poster board strip. Then, draw a leaf on each 6-inch green square, cut it out, and glue it on the flower stem.

One Step More

Cover a bulletin board with light blue paper. Attach a green strip of paper grass along the bottom. Then, add the 3-D sunflowers to create a colorful seasonal display.

Language Arts Link

Use Lola M. Schaefer's *This Is the Sunflower* or Gerald Legg's *From Seed to Sunflower* as a springboard for a discussion about the life cycle of a sunflower. Afterward, give children several half-sheets of paper. On each page, have them illustrate a different stage of a sunflower's life cycle and write a short description about what happens in that stage. When finished, ask them to sequence the pages and bind them between construction-paper covers to create a booklet. Challenge more advanced children to write and perform a skit that tells about the life cycle of a sunflower from the sunflower's point of view.

Related Reading

From Seed to Sunflower by Gerald Legg (Franklin Watts, 1998)

Sunflower House by Eve Bunting (Voyager, 1999)

This Is the Sunflower by Lola M. Schaefer (Greenwillow, 2000)

Silly Summer Insects

Invite children to create these playful critters to reinforce the characteristics of insects.

Art Concepts
primary colors
secondary colors
shape

Let's Begin

Tell children that all insects have six legs and three main body parts—a head, thorax, and abdomen. Then, ask them to name some common insects, such as ants, bees, butterflies, and crickets. Afterward, show children the color wheel and have them name the six colors on it. Point out the primary colors: red, yellow, and blue. Tell them that the other colors (orange, green, and purple) are secondary colors because they are made by mixing together two primary colors. Next, display the completed project. Have children identify the primary and secondary colors on it. Explain that the insect's head, thorax, and abdomen are created from primary colors, while other details, such as the legs and wings, are in secondary colors. Finally, have children identify the shapes in the project.

Tell children that they will create a real or silly summer insect using primary and secondary colors. Pass out the materials and demonstrate the procedures as children follow along.

Materials

To display:
- completed project
- color wheel (page 197)

For each child:
- pencil
- 12- by 18-inch white construction paper
- scissors

To share:
- 6-inch squares of construction paper in red, yellow, and blue
- glue sticks
- scraps of construction paper in green, orange, and purple

Timesaving Tip!
Use a paper cutter to cut the construction paper in the sizes needed for the project. You can stack and cut several sheets of paper at a time.

Step by Step

1. Choose three 6-inch squares of paper in primary colors to use for the head, thorax, and abdomen. The paper can all be the same or different colors. Use pencil to draw a shape for each part of the insect's body on a separate square. You might use circles, squares, ovals, hearts, rectangles, and so on. Each body part might be the same or a different shape. Cut out the three shapes and glue them together on the large white paper.

2. Choose scraps of paper in a secondary color to use for the legs. Draw and cut out six legs. Glue the legs onto the insect.

3. Draw additional features for the insect on secondary colors of scrap paper. You might create wings, eyes, antennae, a stinger, and so on. Glue each piece onto the insect.

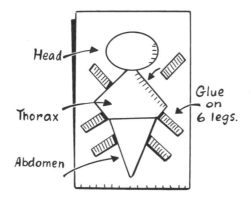

One Step More

Cover a bulletin board with blue or green paper. Display the insects on the board with the title "Interesting Insects."

Language Arts Link

Ask children to cut out a large white speech bubble. Have them write on their speech bubble something that their insect might say to let others know what it is or what it does. For example, they might write "I am a flutterby. I like to flutter over ponds and land on lily pads. My favorite food comes from water lilies." Children might use factual or made-up information in their speech bubble. When finished, display the speech bubbles with their insects. Have more advanced children write a description of their insects to add to the display.

Related Reading

The Best Book of Bugs by Claire Llewellyn (Kingfisher, 1998)

Bugs Are Insects by Anne Rockwell (HarperTrophy, 2001)

Bugs! Bugs! Bugs! by Bob Barner (Chronicle Books, 1999)

Crickwing by Janell Cannon (Harcourt Children's Books, 2000)

Spin-Around Sun

Children can have fun with the sun when they use these movable projects to share their sun knowledge with others.

Art Concepts

shape
line
pattern
warm colors

Materials

To display:
- completed project
- color wheel (page 197)

For each child:
- 6-inch square of red construction paper
- 9-inch square of orange construction paper
- 12-inch square of yellow construction paper
- pencil
- scissors
- brass paper fastener
- fine-tip black permanent marker

To share:
- 12 tagboard circle templates in each of these sizes: 4½-inch, 6-inch, and 8-inch

Let's Begin

Discuss with children facts about the sun, such as the sun is a star, it lights and warms the Earth, and the Earth rotates around the sun. Afterward, show them the completed project. Ask them to describe the kinds of lines and shapes in the project. Do they see any patterns? Tell them that a pattern is formed by repeated lines, shapes, or colors. Then, have children name the colors. Explain that red, yellow, and orange are called warm colors because they suggest warmth. Display the color wheel and have children find the warm colors on it. Why are these appropriate colors to use for the sun? Finally, talk about the facial expression on the project. What mood or emotion does it suggest?

Tell children that they will create a movable sun. Pass out the materials and demonstrate the procedures as children follow along.

TimeSaving Tip!

Use a paper cutter to cut the construction paper squares into the shapes needed for the project. You can stack and cut several sheets of paper at a time.

Step by Step

1. Use pencil to trace the 4½-inch circle template onto the red square. Trace the 6-inch circle onto the orange square and the 8-inch circle onto the yellow square. Then, using the penciled circles as a guide, use the black marker to create a decorative rim around each circle. You might use zigzag, curvy, scalloped, or castle-top lines. Use a different kind of line for each circle. Cut out each circle along the decorative line.

Cut out circles along lines.

2. Stack the cutouts with the red on top and yellow on bottom. Then, push the paper fastener through the center of the stack of cutouts to attach the three pieces together.

Fastener

3. Place the three-colored sun on the table. Use the marker to trace the rim of the red cutout onto the orange one. Be sure to hold the red cutout steady so that it doesn't move while you're tracing. Then, trace the rim of the orange cutout onto the outer yellow one.

4. Draw a face on the red center of the sun. You might draw a happy, silly, or surprised expression on the face.

5. Use pencil to draw a repeating pattern of shapes around the rims of the orange and yellow cutouts. Use 1–3 simple shapes, such as diamonds, hearts, or stars. You can draw a different pattern on each of the colored pieces. Trace the patterns with the black marker.

6. Spin the red and orange sections of the sun to give the sun a variety of interesting looks. You can spin each piece separately and in the same or different directions.

One Step More

Trace the pattern around the rim of the yellow section with red or orange glitter crayons or glitter glue.

Language Arts Link

Write *spin* and *sun* on chart paper and have children say the words aloud. Explain that each of these words belongs to a word family. Underline the ending of each word to show children what word family it belongs to. Then, ask them to call out words that belong to the same word families, such as *chin, grin, pin, bun, fun,* and *run.* Write each of their responses under the corresponding word on the chart. Afterward, have them create sun-related sentences and rhymes using words from the two word family lists. Ask more advanced children to use the word family words to write a short rhyme or create words to sing to the tune of familiar songs.

Related Reading

The Sun...Our Nearest Star by Franklyn M. Branley (HarperTrophy, 2002)

The Sun Is Always Shining Somewhere by Allan Fowler (Children's Press, 1992)

Sun Up, Sun Down by Gail Gibbons (Voyager Books, 1987)

The Sun Is My Favorite Star by Frank Asch (Gulliver Books, 2000)

Wild and Wonderful Sunglasses

Use this fun project to reinforce sun safety practices and encourage children to protect their eyes from the sun.

Materials

To display:

• completed project

For each child:

• 4- by 7-inch sheet of tagboard

• two 3- by 6-inch strips of tagboard

• pencil

• scissors

• color markers

To share:

• 8 tagboard sunglass frame templates of each shape (page 190)

• 12 tagboard earpiece templates (page 190)

• glue sticks

• 2-inch squares of cellophane in assorted colors (two squares per child)

Let's Begin

Discuss sun safety practices with children, including the importance of protecting their eyes from the sun. Then, show them the completed project. Ask them to name the colors on the sunglasses. What kinds of lines and shapes were used to decorate the project? Do children see a pattern? Explain that a pattern is created by repeating colors, lines, or shapes. Next, point out the colored cellophane used for the lenses of the sunglasses. Tell children that this material does not provide adequate protection from the sun and that the project should not be worn as eye protection while in the sun.

Tell children that they will make their own pair of wild and wonderful sunglasses. Pass out the materials, then demonstrate the procedures as children follow along.

Timesaving Tip!

Use a paper cutter to cut the tagboard to the sizes needed for the project. You can stack and cut several sheets of tagboard at a time.

Step by Step

1. Decide what shape to use for the front frame of your sunglasses. Choose that template and trace it with pencil onto the 4- by 7-inch tagboard. (Or draw the shape of your choice to use for the frame.) Then, trace the earpiece template onto the two 3- by 6-inch tagboard strips.

2. Cut out the sunglass frame and the earpieces. Be sure to cut out the openings in the frame.

3. Use pencil to draw a pattern of lines, shapes, or a combination of the two on the frame and both earpieces. To add interest, you might draw one kind of pattern on the frame and a different pattern on the earpieces (be sure to draw an identical pattern on both earpieces). Use color markers to color the patterns.

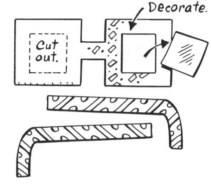

Decorate.

Cut out.

4. Choose two squares of cellophane in the color of your choice. Both squares might be the same or different colors. Glue one cellophane square to the back of each opening in your sunglass frame. Then, trim the cellophane to fit the shape.

5. Glue an earpiece to each side of the frame. Fold the earpieces and place the sunglasses on your face.

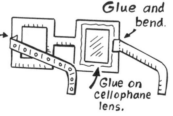

Glue and bend.

Glue on cellophane lens.

One Step More

For sturdier sunglasses, cut out a second tagboard frame. Then, glue it to the back of the decorated frame so that the cellophane lenses and earpiece ends are sandwiched between the two frames.

Language Arts Link

Explain that *sunglasses* is a compound word. Write the two words that make up this word on the chalkboard. Then, challenge children to brainstorm other compound words that contain the word *sun*, such as *sunshine, sunlight, sunroof,* and *sunset.* Write their responses on the board. Afterward, ask children to write *sun* at the top of a large sheet of construction paper. Have them write on their paper at least five words from the board, illustrate the words, and then circle *sun* in each one. Challenge more advanced children to create sun safety posters, using as many of the compound words from the list as possible.

Related Reading

Fun Dog, Sun Dog by Deborah Heiligman (Marshall Cavendish Children's Books, 2005)

Lilly's Purple Plastic Purse by Kevin Henkes (Greenwillow, 1996)

The Sunglass Kid by Leslie L. Spradlin (Booksurge, 2005)

Sensational Sun Visor

Invite children to create these fashionable sun visors to use while practicing sun safety practices.

Art Concepts
color
line
shape
alternating pattern

Materials

To display:
- completed project

For each child:
- 9- by 12-inch tagboard
- pencil
- scissors
- 1- by 18-inch strip of tagboard
- fine-tip black permanent marker
- color markers

To share:
- 12 sun visor templates (page 191)
- glue sticks

Let's Begin

Tell children that a sun visor shields their eyes from the sun and keeps their face shaded to prevent sunburn. Then, show them the completed project. Have them name the different colors used in the project. What kinds of lines and shapes decorate the sun visor? Are any of the colors, lines, or shapes repeated? Explain that when any of these elements are repeated, a pattern is created. An alternating pattern occurs when a series of two or more elements, such as a circle and square, is repeated. Point out the alternating pattern on the project.

Tell children that they will create a sun visor decorated with an alternating pattern. Pass out the materials and demonstrate the procedures as children follow along.

Timesaving Tip!

Use a paper cutter to cut the tagboard strips for the project. You can stack and cut several sheets of tagboard at a time.

Step by Step

1. Use pencil to trace the sun visor template onto the tagboard. Cut out the shape.

2. To make a border, draw a line that parallels and is about ½ inch away from the outer curve of the cutout. Then, pencil in an alternating pattern in the border. You might use lines, shapes, or both, but be sure to repeat the pattern along the entire border.

3. Draw a sun in the middle of the cutout. To create the rays around the sun, draw an alternating pattern of short and long lines, lines and triangles, or any other combination of elements that give the appearance of sunrays. Then, add facial features to the sun.

4. For the sun visor strap, use pencil to draw an alternating pattern on the tagboard strip. The pattern might be identical to or different from the one on the border of the sun visor.

5. Use the black fine-tip marker to trace all the drawings on the sun visor and strap. Then, color the drawings with the color markers.

6. Glue one end of the strap to the sun visor, as shown. Ask a friend to help you measure and trim the strap to fit your head before gluing the other end to the sun visor.

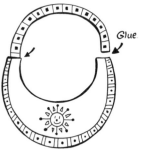

Glue

One Step More

Use clothespins to hang the sun visors across a clothesline in the classroom. Invite children to remove their sun visors from the clothesline and wear them when they go outdoors for recess.

Language Arts Link

Write *visor* at the top of a sheet of chart paper. Say the word and have children identify the name and sound of the first letter. Then, ask them to brainstorm as many words as possible that begin with *v*, such as *van, vest, vine,* and *volcano*. After writing their responses on the chart, review the words with children. Then, say one word at a time, some beginning with *v* and others beginning with other sounds, including *f*. Ask children to form a V with their fingers and hold it up in the air each time they hear a *v* word. Have more advanced children write sentences using two or more *v* words in each sentence.

Related Reading

Do You Have a Hat? by Eileen Spinelli (Simon & Schuster, 2004)

Hetty's 100 Hats by Janet Slingsby (Good Books, 2005)

Fun in the Sun Safely by Dianne Goldman-York (York Goldman Enterprises, 2005)

Fancy Flip-Flops

*Step into math fun with this fancy footwear project
that can be used to reinforce shapes, patterns, and counting.*

Art Concepts
line
shape
alternating pattern

Materials

To display:
- completed project

For each child:
- 9- by 12-inch sheet of tagboard
- pencil
- scissors
- fine-tip black permanent marker
- two 16-inch lengths of yarn

To share:
- 12 tagboard flip-flop templates (page 192)
- hole punch
- oil pastels (one box for every two children)
- tape

Let's Begin

Ask for a show of hands from children who have a pair of flip-flops. Invite them to describe the kinds of designs used to decorate their flip-flops. Then, show children the completed project. Point out the lines and shapes in the design. Ask them if they see a pattern. Explain that a pattern is created by repeating lines, shapes, or colors. An alternating pattern occurs when a series of two or more elements, such as a dot and diamond, is repeated. Call children's attention to the alternating pattern on the project. Then, choose a shape on the flip-flops and count with children the number of times that shape occurs in the design on one shoe.

Tell children that they will create a pair of fancy flip-flops. Pass out the materials and demonstrate the procedures as children follow along.

Timesaving Tip!
Precut the tagboard flip-flops and punch the holes in each one. Then, have children start at Step 2 to make the project.

Step by Step

1. Use pencil to trace the flip-flop template twice onto the sheet of tagboard. Mark through the holes in the template to show the hole placement on the tagboard outlines. Cut out each shape. Use a hole punch to punch the three holes in each cutout.

2. Pencil in an alternating pattern on the cutouts. You might use lines, shapes, or both, but be sure to draw the same pattern on both cutouts. Use the black fine-tip marker to trace the patterns and then color them with the oil pastels.

3. For each flip-flop strap, fold a length of yarn in half. Tie a knot in the yarn about 2 inches from the fold. Then, poke the looped end through the hole at the top of the flip-flop and tape the end to the back. Poke each loose end of the yarn through a hole on the side of the shoe and tape the ends in place.

← Knot.

← Tape ends to bottom.

One Step More

Tie the two flip-flops together with a short length of yarn laced through the holes at the arches. Then, write a message on the back and use as a greeting card for Mother's Day, Father's Day, or another special occasion.

Summer

Language Arts Link

Read *Flip Flop Bop* by Matt Novak. Then, work with children to make a list of action words used in the story (such as *skipping, hopping,* and *dropping*). Explain that these words are called verbs because they describe actions. Invite children to add other verbs to the list. Afterward, call out one word at a time from the list and have children act it out. More advanced children might make a list of verbs that begin with *fl* (the same sound at the beginning of *flip-flop*). Then, have them write each word in a sentence and illustrate it.

Related Reading

Beach Day by Karen Roosa (Clarion Books, 2001)

Flip Flop Bop by Matt Novak (Roaring Brook Press, 2005)

Whose Slippers Are Those? by Marilyn Kahalewai (Bess Press, 2005)

- 143 -

Textured Zoo Animals

Use these textured critters as part of a zoo unit to reinforce children's knowledge of zoo animals and the workers that care for them.

Art Concepts
shape
visual texture
tactile texture

Materials

To display:
- completed project
- texture reference chart (page 199)

For each child:
- pencil
- fine-tip black permanent marker
- scissors

To share:
- 12- by 18-inch construction paper in assorted colors
- oil pastels (one box for every two children)
- glue sticks

Let's Begin

Invite children to tell about their experiences at the zoo. What kind of animals did they see there? After sharing, show them the completed project. Point out the shape of the zoo animal. Then, call their attention to the textured cuts in its body. Explain that the cuts create visual texture because they make the animal appear to have texture. The cuts also give the animal tactile texture because the texture can be felt by rubbing a hand over the surface of the animal. Afterward, show children the texture reference chart. Ask them to find designs on the chart that might make an animal have the appearance of texture. Talk about the lines and shapes that are used to create the different kinds of texture.

Tell children that they will create a textured zoo animal. Pass out the materials and demonstrate the procedures as children follow along.

Timesaving Tip!
Provide large tagboard shape templates for children to trace for their animal bodies.

Step by Step

1. Decide what kind of zoo animal to draw. Then, choose the paper in the color you want to use for the animal. Using pencil, draw a large shape in the middle of the paper to use for the animal's body. Be sure to use a basic shape such as a circle, oval, triangle, square, rectangle, or half-oval. Add a head, legs, and other details to the animal, leaving the large body blank.

2. Trace the pencil drawing with the black marker. Then, cut out the animal.

3. To texture the body, make a horizontal or vertical fold near one end of the animal's body. Cut several short lines into the fold. You might cut straight, curved, or angled lines. Be sure not to cut too deep into the fold to avoid cutting away parts of the animal. Then, unfold and flatten the cutout. It will have short slits along the fold line.

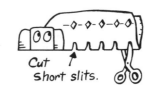

Cut short slits.

4. Fold another section of the animal's body parallel to the first fold and make cuts similar to the first set of cuts. Continue folding and cutting until the entire body of the animal has been textured in this manner.

5. Unfold and flatten the animal cutout. Choose the color paper that you want to use for the background. Glue the animal to the paper, making sure to glue down the body only around the edges. Then, fold up the paper at all the slits in the body.

6. Use oil pastels to color in the animal's facial features and other details.

One Step More

Use the black marker to draw a simple scene on the background around the animal. Color the scene with oil pastels.

Language Arts Link

Talk about some of the many animals children might see at a zoo. List the animal names on chart paper. Then, invite children to play animal charades. To play, children take turns whispering to you an animal listed on the chart. They act out their chosen zoo animal, without giving away its name. When the others guess the animal, the actor points out the name of the animal on the list. After playing, ask more advanced children to create a short story about zoo life, writing from their animal's perspective. Invite them to share their stories with the class.

Related Reading

Going to the Zoo by Tom Paxton (HarperCollins, 1996)

If Anything Ever Goes Wrong at the Zoo by Mary Jean Hendrick (Voyager Books, 1996)

My Visit to the Zoo by Aliki (HarperTrophy, 1999)

Our Class Took a Trip to the Zoo by Shirley Neitzel (Greenwillow, 2002)

Blue-Water Fishbowl

Use this colorful project to acquaint children with a variety of fish and their underwater world.

Art Concepts

color
shape
texture

Materials

To display:

- pictures of different kinds of fish (see Related Reading for books featuring pictures of fish)
- completed project
- texture reference chart (page 199)

For each child:

- 12- by 18-inch gray construction paper
- scissors
- 12- by 18-inch white construction paper
- pencil
- fine-tip black permanent marker
- fluorescent and regular color markers
- 12- by 18-inch sheet of blue plastic wrap

To share:

- 12 tagboard fishbowl templates (page 193)
- glue sticks

Let's Begin

Display the fish pictures and the completed project. Ask children to share what they know about the characteristics of fish. Do they have pet fish at home? After sharing, talk about the colors and shapes of the fish in the displayed items. Then, point out how the designs on the fish in the project give them a textured appearance. Explain that the appearance of texture makes the fish look more realistic. Finally, show children the texture reference chart, and ask them to find designs that might resemble the texture of a fish.

Tell children that they will create a fishbowl containing colorful fish. Pass out the materials. Then, demonstrate the procedures as children follow along.

Timesaving Tip!

To glue the blue plastic wrap to the fishbowl frame, ask children to tape the corners of their sheets to the table. Have them apply glue to the frame, turn it over, and press it firmly onto the plastic wrap.

Step by Step

1. Fold the light gray paper in half lengthwise. Place the fishbowl template with the straight edges along the fold and use pencil to trace the template. Cut out the shape and unfold the cutout to reveal a frame in the shape of a fishbowl.

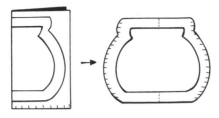

2. Place the fishbowl frame in the middle of the white paper. Use pencil to carefully trace around the inside opening of the fishbowl. Then, set the cutout aside.

3. In pencil, draw several fish inside the fishbowl outline. The fish might be in different shapes and sizes and have designs such as large vertical stripes, spots, or other kinds of lines and shapes. As you draw, be sure to include designs that give texture to the appearance of the fish. You can refer to the texture reference chart to find designs that resemble the texture of fish. If desired, include additional drawings of things that might be found in a fishbowl, such as small plants and rocks.

4. Trace all the drawings with the black marker and then color them with the color markers.

5. Glue the blue plastic wrap to the gray fishbowl frame. Trim the plastic to the outer edges of the frame. Then, place the frame over the fish drawings, aligning the inside of the frame with the fishbowl outline on the white paper. Glue the frame in place.

Frame with plastic wrap.

One Step More

Cut out the entire fishbowl from the white paper. Then, display the fishbowls on a bulletin board titled "Our Fabulous Fish."

Language Arts Link

Write *fish* on chart paper. Say the word with children, have them listen to the word ending, and then underline the ending sound. Explain that *fish* belongs to a family of words that end with this same sound. Invite children to brainstorm other words that belong to the *fish* word family, such as *dish, squish,* and *wish*. Write their responses on the chart. Afterward, have them write fish-related rhymes using words from the list. Ask more advanced children to write a rhyme about each fish in their fishbowl. If desired, display the rhymes with children's fishbowl projects.

Related Reading

The Birthday Fish by Dan Yaccarino (Henry Holt and Company, 2005)

Hooray for Fish! by Lucy Cousins (Candlewick, 2005)

Mr. Putter & Tabby Feed the Fish by Cynthia Rylant (Harcourt, 2002)

Trout, Trout, Trout: A Fish Chant by April Pulley Sayre (Northwood Press, 2004)

Cool Summer Salad

Emphasize healthy eating habits with this colorful salad that looks both nutritious and delicious.

Art Concepts
color
shape
texture

Materials

To display:
- completed project
- texture reference chart (page 199)

For each child:
- 4- by 9-inch purple construction paper
- pencil
- scissors
- fine-tip black permanent marker
- 9- by 12-inch light gray construction paper

To share:
- 3- by 6-inch sheets of light and medium green crepe paper
- scraps of construction paper in assorted colors
- glue sticks

Let's Begin

Show children the completed project. Ask them to tell what the project represents and what foods they recognize in it. Explain that salads are often included in a healthy diet and usually contain colorful and tasty foods. Then, have children name the colors and shapes used in the project. Do any of the foods appear to have texture? Explain that artists use lines and other designs to give their work texture and help make it appear more realistic. Then, show children the texture reference chart. Ask children to find designs that might resemble the appearance, or texture, of foods found in a salad.

Tell children that they will create a summer salad. Pass out the materials and demonstrate the procedures as children follow along.

Timesaving Tip!

Use a paper cutter to cut the construction and crepe paper in the sizes needed for the project.

Step by Step

1. To make a salad plate, use pencil to draw a large oval on the 4- by 9-inch purple paper. Cut out the shape, then draw an oval inside the shape about an inch from the rim. Trace the oval with the black marker.

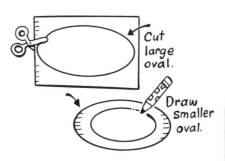

Cut large oval.

Draw smaller oval.

2. Place the 9- by 12-inch gray paper vertically on the table. Glue the purple cutout onto the paper about 2 inches from the bottom.

3. Cut out several large lettuce leaf shapes from the light and medium green crepe paper. Apply glue to the middle of the leaves and glue them onto the salad plate. Position the leaves so that they overlap, but also appear to be spread out on the plate. To give the lettuce a more realistic look, gently stretch and fluff the edges of the crepe paper leaves.

Glue "lettuce" to plate.

4. Use pencil to draw different kinds of salad foods on scrap paper in the colors of your choice. You might draw red tomato slices, orange carrot sticks, green cucumber wedges, purple onion strips, and so on. Be sure to add designs that give texture to the foods and make them look more realistic. Finally, trace each drawing and its details with the black marker, cut out each piece, and glue the cutouts onto and around the lettuce leaves to resemble salad in a dish.

One Step More

Mount the salad picture on 12- by 18-inch yellow construction paper. Then, add it to a bulletin board display titled "Sensational Summer Salads."

Language Arts Link

Tell children that salads are made of foods that go together, such as lettuce and tomatoes. Then, have them name go-together word pairs such as *sock* and *shoe* and *paper* and *pencil*. Write the word pairs on the chalkboard. Invite children to create a word salad with the pairs. To begin, have them cut out several pairs of shapes and then write each word in a go-together pair on identical shapes. Next, they can glue the shapes collage-style onto a drawing of a plate. When finished, ask children to read the words in their salads and tell which pairs go together. Have more advanced children write riddles about words in the go-together pairs.

Related Reading

An Alphabet Salad: Fruits and Vegetables from A to Z by Sarah L. Schuette (Capstone, 2003)

I Will Never Not Ever Eat a Tomato by Lauren Child (Candlewick, 2003)

Showdown at the Food Pyramid by Rex Barron (Putnam Juvenile, 2004)

Woven Patriotic Banner

Use these red, white, and blue banners to wrap up a unit on the American flag.

Art Concepts

color
shape
line
pattern

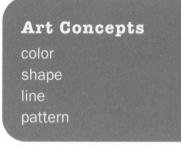

Materials

To display:
- American flag, or a picture of one (see Related Reading for books featuring flag pictures)
- completed project

For each child:
- 9- by 12-inch white construction paper
- pencil
- ruler
- scissors

To share:
- 1- by 12-inch strips of red construction paper (about eight per child)
- glue sticks
- scraps of blue construction paper
- silver or white star stickers

Let's Begin

Show children the flag pictures and completed project. Ask them to name the colors and shapes in the pictures and project. Explain that the official colors of the American flag are red, white, and blue, and that the flag is often referred to as the "Stars and Stripes" because of the shapes and lines on it. Ask children to describe the kinds of horizontal and vertical lines found on the project. Draw their attention to the woven pattern of the banner. Explain that this pattern was created by weaving red strips of paper through cuts in the white paper. Finally, tell them that a pattern is created by repeating lines, colors, or shapes. What lines, shapes, or colors are repeated on the banner?

Tell children that they will create a patriotic banner from red, white, and blue paper. Pass out the materials and demonstrate the procedures as children follow along.

Timesaving Tip!

Use a paper cutter to cut the red construction paper strips for the project. You can stack and cut several sheets of paper at a time.

Step by Step

1. Fold the white paper in half horizontally. Use a pencil to draw a vertical line about one ruler width away from the edge opposite the fold. Then, draw five horizontal lines from the fold to the vertical line. You can use straight, curvy, or zigzag lines.

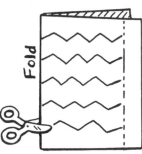

2. Cut along each horizontal line, starting at the fold and stopping at the vertical line. Be sure to cut through both layers of the folded paper. Open the paper to reveal the five horizontal cuts in it.

3. Weave the red paper strips in an over-and-under motion through the horizontal cuts in the white paper. Alternate the weaving pattern for each strip. Slide the strips close together so that you can weave as many strips as possible into the white paper.

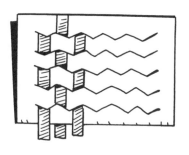

4. Line up and glue the top of each red strip to the top of the white paper. Let the red strips extend beyond the bottom of the white paper.

5. To add blue to the banner, draw a shape on a scrap of blue paper. You might draw a circle, square, rectangle, or any other shape of your choice. Cut out the shape and glue it onto the banner in any location you desire.

6. Add stars to the banner. You might stick a star at the end of each red strip, create a design on the blue shape, or edge the white paper with stars.

One Step More

Display the patriotic banners around a bulletin board, over door and window frames, or across the top of walls in the classroom.

Language Arts Link

Tell children that the American flag is often displayed with pride. Write *flag* and *pride* on chart paper and underline the two-letter blend at the beginning of each word. Ask children to brainstorm other words that begin with *fl* and *pr*, such as *flap, fly, press,* and *prop*. List their responses on the chart. Then, have children draw a tally mark next to each word on the list as they come across it in their reading activities. If they find a new word that begins with *fl* or *pr*, have them add it to the list. At the end of the day, count to see which word appeared most often in children's reading material. Have more advanced children write and illustrate sentences using words from the list.

Related Reading

F Is For Flag by Wendy Cheyette Lewison (Grosset & Dunlap, 2002)

The Flag We Love by Pam Munoz Ryan (Charlesbridge Publishing, 2006)

The Pledge of Allegiance (Scholastic Inc., 2001)

Stars and Stripes: The Story of the American Flag by Sarah L. Thomson (HarperCollins, 2003)

Stretchin' Uncle Sam

Use these patriotic projects to stretch children's knowledge of Independence Day symbols and traditions.

Art Concepts

color
line
shape
pattern

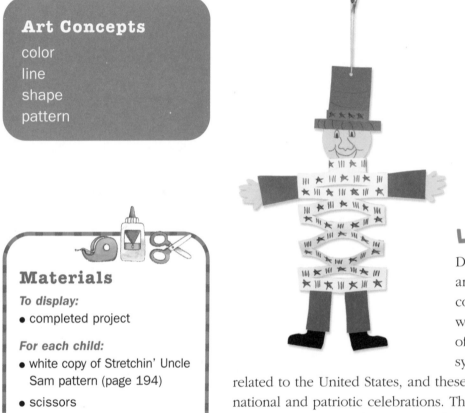

Materials

To display:
- completed project

For each child:
- white copy of Stretchin' Uncle Sam pattern (page 194)
- scissors
- pencil
- fine-tip black permanent marker
- crayons

To share:
- glue sticks
- twelve 3½-inch tagboard circle templates
- 4-inch squares of construction paper in assorted flesh colors
- 5-inch squares of red and blue construction paper
- scraps of construction paper in red, white, blue, and assorted flesh colors

Let's Begin

Display the completed project and have children name the colors in it. Point out that red, white, and blue are the colors of the American flag. Each color symbolizes an important concept related to the United States, and these colors are often used in national and patriotic celebrations. Then, ask children to describe the kinds of lines and shapes used in the project. Gently bounce Uncle Sam up and down so that it stretches. Explain that his body was created by cutting straight lines across a sheet of paper. Inform children that a pattern is created by a repeating line, color, or shape. Have them examine the project to find and describe the patterns they see.

Tell children that they will create a stretching Uncle Sam. Pass out the materials and demonstrate the procedures as children follow along.

Timesaving Tip!

Use a paper cutter to cut the construction paper in the sizes needed for the project. You can stack and cut several sheets of paper at a time.

Step by Step

1. Cut out the body pattern and place it facedown on the table. Use pencil to draw one or more patterns on the cutout. You might cover the cutout with an alternating pattern that includes elements on the American flag, such as stars and stripes. Or you might use a variety of lines and shapes to create several patterns.

2. Trace the drawings with the black marker, then color them with the red and blue crayons.

3. Turn the cutout over with the lines faceup and fold it along the middle line so that the patterned side is inside. Cut along each horizontal line through both layers of the paper. When finished, unfold the paper and place it with the colored side up.

4. To make Uncle Sam's collar, glue together the ends of the top section of the body to create a tube.

5. For the head, trace the circle template onto a 4-inch square of flesh-colored paper. Cut out the circle, draw a face on it, and glue it to the collar, as shown.

6. Choose three 5-inch squares of paper. Use pencil to draw a large hat on one square, then fold the other two squares in half. Draw arms for Uncle Sam on one folded square and legs on the other. Cut out all the shapes, making sure to cut the arms and legs through both layers of paper. Glue each piece onto the body.

7. Cut out hands, shoes, and other details from scraps of paper. Glue on each piece.

Pattern inside

Cut each line.

Glue ends.

One Step More

Attach a yarn hanger to the top of the project. Then, suspend the Stretchin' Uncle Sam for others to enjoy.

Language Arts Link

Write *stretch* on chart paper, say the word, and underline the blend at the beginning of it. Ask children to name other words that begin with *str*, such as *straw*, *street*, *stripe*, and *strong*. List their responses on chart paper. Then, have children create a booklet about an imaginary Independence Day activity such as a parade. Ask them to use as many *str* words from the list as possible in their story. Challenge more advanced children to include alliterative sentences using *str* words in their stories. Afterward, invite children to share their booklets with the class.

Related Reading

Happy 4th of July, Jenny Sweeney by Leslie Kimmelman (Albert Whitman & Company, 2003)

Happy Birthday, America by Mary Pope Osborne (Roaring Brook Press, 2005)

Hooray for the Fourth of July by Wendy Watson (Clarion Books, 2000)

Fourth of July Celebration

Invite children to create these brilliant pictures to celebrate the traditional fireworks that light up the sky on the Fourth of July.

Art Concepts

line
shape
overlap

Materials

To display:
- completed project

For each child:
- 12- by 18-inch dark blue construction paper
- pencil
- oil pastels

For the paint station:
- white, orange, yellow, peach and medium blue tempera paint
- 10 small Styrofoam plates
- cotton swabs

Let's Begin

Tell children that most Fourth of July celebrations end with a fireworks display. Invite them to share their experiences with fireworks shows. Then, display the completed project. Ask children to describe the different kinds of lines in the project, such as curvy, spiraling, swirling, and broken lines. What shapes do they see? Point out how some of the objects are partially hidden behind other objects. Explain that artists use this technique—called overlapping—to help give their work a more realistic appearance. Finally, tell children that the brilliant colors that create the fireworks in the project were applied with a nontraditional art material—cotton swabs!

Inform children that they will create a picture of a fireworks show. Pass out the materials and demonstrate the procedures as children follow along.

Timesaving Tip!

Set up the paint station ahead of time. Cover a large table with newspaper, then place the Styrofoam plates and cotton swabs on the table. Just before beginning the activity, pour a layer of paint into each plate, using two plates for each color.

Step by Step

1. Place the blue paper horizontally on the table. Use a pencil to draw a skyline on the bottom half of the paper. You might include a variety of shapes to represent buildings, trees, and other objects. Be sure to overlap some of the objects in the drawing.

2. Use a black oil pastel to trace the outlines of the objects in the drawing. Then, use other colors of oil pastels to color in the picture.

3. Take the picture to the paint station. Use cotton swabs dipped in white, orange, or yellow paint to draw fireworks in the sky. You might draw swirls, spirals, waves, broken lines, and fountain-like sprays of lines to represent the fireworks. Be sure to use a different cotton swab for each paint color.

4. To create accents in the sky, use a cotton swab and medium blue paint to outline the fireworks and to add wavy or connecting lines to the display.

One Step More

Display the projects on a bulletin board covered with black paper.

Language Arts Link

Write *four* on chart paper. Read the word and then write the word for each numeral from 1–12. Have children read the words together. Then, point to one number word at a time. Invite a volunteer to read the word and write the corresponding numeral on the chart. Afterward, have children create number mini-posters. To begin, ask them to write all the number words from the chart on a large sheet of construction paper. Then, have them write the corresponding numeral beside each word and draw a picture that depicts that number (for example, they might draw an octopus for *eight*). Invite children to share their mini-posters with the class. Challenge more advanced children to use the number words to write number rhymes or songs.

Related Reading

Apple Pie Fourth of July by Janet S. Wong (Voyager Books, 2006)

Fourth of July Mice! by Bethany Roberts (Clarion, 2004)

The Fourth of July Story by Alice Dalgliesh (Aladdin, 1987)

Patchwork Elephant Puzzle

Children can use these patchwork pachyderms to reinforce skills in patterning, counting, and geometry.

Art Concepts
line
shape
pattern

Materials

To display:
- completed project

For each child:
- pencil
- fine-tip black permanent markers
- color markers

To share:
- one tagboard elephant puzzle for every six children, with the number for each piece labeled on the back (page 195)

Let's Begin

Display the six pieces of the completed project in a random array. Invite children to describe the lines and shapes used on the puzzle pieces. Explain that a pattern is created when one or more elements, such as line and shape, are repeated. Point out one puzzle piece at a time. Do children see a pattern on that piece? Invite a volunteer to describe the pattern. Next, draw children's attention to the shape of each puzzle piece. What do they think the pieces will create when assembled? After sharing, put the puzzle together, starting with the elephant's head. When finished, explain that the assembled puzzle is a patchwork elephant.

Tell children that they will create a puzzle piece for a patchwork elephant puzzle. Divide the class into groups of six and give each child a tagboard puzzle piece (if needed, give extra pieces to some children to make sure all six pieces of a puzzle are decorated). Pass out the materials and demonstrate the procedures as children follow along.

Timesaving Tip!

For the puzzle pieces, top several sheets of 12- by 18-inch tagboard with an enlarged copy of the elephant pattern. Cut out the puzzle pieces through all the layers. Number each piece as shown on the pattern.

Step by Step

1. Place the puzzle piece on the table with the number side down. Use pencil to draw a pattern on the piece. You can use the same kind of line or shape to create the pattern. Or you might draw a repeating pattern of two or three kinds of lines or shapes. If desired, you can draw a pattern using a combination of lines and shapes.

2. Trace the pattern with the black marker, then use other markers to color the pattern.

3. When all the members of your group finish decorating their puzzle pieces, put the puzzle together. Talk about the different patterns used in the patchwork design of the puzzle. Later, you might find a child in another group who has the same puzzle number as yours, switch places with that child, and add your piece to the new group's puzzle.

One Step More

Laminate all the puzzle pieces. Then, group together the pieces for each puzzle, put each group in a separate resealable plastic bag, and place the puzzle bags in the math center.

Language Arts Link

Ask children to say *elephant* and tell what short vowel they hear at the beginning of the word. Have them brainstorm other words that contain the short *e* sound, such as *bed, fell, get, men,* and *rest.* Write their responses on the board and then review the words with children. Ask volunteers to underline the letter that makes the short *e* sound in each word. Afterward, have children use short *e* words from the list to create elephant-related rhymes. Ask more advanced children to sort the one-syllable short *e* words into word family groups. Challenge them to add as many more words as possible to each group.

Related Reading

Ella the Elegant Elephant by Carmela D'Amico (Arthur A. Levine Books, 2004)

Elmer by David McKee (HarperCollins, 1989)

Emma Kate by Patricia Polacco (Philomel, 2005)

The Quilt by Ann Jonas (Puffin, 1994)

Circus Clown

Wrap up a study about the circus with these picture-perfect clown portraits.

Art Concepts
color
shape
pattern

Materials

To display
- completed project

For each child:
- 12- by 18-inch white construction paper
- pencil
- black marker
- color markers
- scissors

To share:
- 4- by 6-inch strips of turquoise, magenta, yellow, green, red, and orange bulletin board paper (five strips for every child)
- glue sticks

Let's Begin

Ask children who have been to a circus to share their experiences and describe the clowns. Then, show them the completed project. Explain that circus clowns often use bright colors and bold, exaggerated shapes in their makeup, clothing, and accessories. Have children name the colors and shapes used in the portrait. Point out how colors are used to emphasize and enlarge the clown's features. Shapes of different sizes also help define and draw attention to different features of the clown. Tell children that patterns create additional interest and an air of silliness to a clown's attire. Explain that patterns are created by repeating lines, shapes, and colors. Have children point out and describe the patterns in the portrait.

Tell children that they will create a circus clown portrait. Pass out the materials, then demonstrate the procedures as children follow along.

Timesaving Tip!

Use a paper cutter to cut the 4- by 6-inch strips of bulletin board paper. You can stack and cut several sheets of paper at a time.

Step by Step

1. Place the white paper vertically on the table. Use pencil to draw a circle about twice the size of a quarter in the middle of the paper. This will be the clown's nose. Draw a large oval head around the nose.

2. Draw two same-shaped eyes above the nose. You might use ovals, stars, diamonds, triangles, or any other shape of your choice. Draw a large banana-shaped mouth below the nose, and add an ear, in the shape of half a peanut shell, on each side of the head. You might also add eyebrows, cheeks, and hair.

3. For clothing, draw a large bowtie just below the oval head, then top the head with a hat. Pencil in a pattern of shapes, lines, or both on the clothing. If desired, add other accessories such as a flower, buttons, and so on.

4. Trace the drawing with the black marker, then color it with color markers. Use bold, bright colors for the facial features and contrasting colors for the clothes and accessories.

5. For the frame, choose five strips of paper in the same color. Use pencil to draw a wavy, zigzag, castle-top, or other type of decorative line down the middle of one strip. Stack

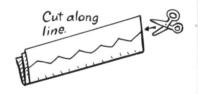

Cut along line.

two strips behind this one and cut along the line through all layers. Then, place one of the cut strips onto an uncut strip, trace along the decorative line, stack the two uncut strips together, and cut along the line. Glue the straight edges of the strips along the edges of the portrait to frame it.

One Step More

Use the clown portraits to border a circus-related bulletin board.

Language Arts Link

Write *circus* on chart paper. Say the word and point out the hard and soft sounds of *c* in it. Then, write several words that begin with each of these sounds on the chart. For example, you might write *can* and *cup* for hard *c* and *cent* and *circle* for soft *c*. Invite children to add other words for each sound. Afterward, have them make simple clown stick puppets. Then, say one word at a time from the list. If the word begins with a hard *c*, children hold up their clown (which begins with hard *c*). If the word begins with soft *c*, they leave their clown at rest. More advanced children might make flash cards to use to practice reading the words and identifying the beginning sounds.

Related Reading

Circus by Lois Ehlert (HarperCollins, 1992)

Emeline at the Circus by Marjorie Priceman (Knopf Books for Young Readers, 1999)

Last Night I Dreamed a Circus by Maya Gottfried (Knopf Books for Young Readers, 2003)

Crescent Critters

Reinforce shape and spatial concepts with these interesting critters constructed from crescents in various sizes.

Art Concepts

shape
texture
overlap

Materials

To display:
- completed project

For each child:
- 12- by 18-inch white construction paper
- pencil

To share:
- 6 tagboard crescent templates of each size (page 196)
- scraps of construction paper in assorted colors
- scissors
- glue sticks

For sponge-printing stations:
- twelve 1-inch square sponges
- shallow trays of white, black, gray, brown, green, and yellow tempera paint

Let's Begin

Draw a crescent on the chalkboard and ask children to name the shape. Explain that it is a crescent—one of the shapes of the moon. Then, show them the completed project. Explain that the critter was created from crescents of different sizes. Sketch out a crescent critter on the board similar to the project. Point out the different crescents that were used to form the critter, such as its body, head, and legs. Tell children that some of the shapes are partially hidden by others. This technique, called overlapping, was used to give the critter a more realistic appearance. Explain that the uneven coloring, which was created with sponge-prints, makes the creature appear to have texture.

Tell children that they will sponge print crescent shapes to create a critter of their choice. Pass out the materials. Then, demonstrate the procedures as children follow along.

Timesaving Tip!

Set up the sponge-printing stations ahead of time. Cover three tables with newspaper. Add a half-inch layer of moist paper towels to six paint trays, then place two trays and four sponges on each table. Just before beginning the activity, spread a different paint color onto the towels in each tray.

Step by Step

1. Decide what critter to make. Then, choose a crescent template in the size of your choice to use for the body. Use pencil to lightly trace the template onto the white paper. You can trace the shape any number of times or in any orientation to achieve the body shape and size desired for your critter.

2. Choose another crescent template to trace for the head. Trace additional templates in the sizes of your choice to create legs, ears, tails, and other features for the critter. Overlap the shapes as needed to achieve the basic shape you want your critter to have. (The overlapping lines will be hidden by the sponge-prints in the next step.)

3. Take your critter to the sponge-printing stations. Fill in the crescents with the paint color of your choice. Then, set the project aside to dry.

4. Draw additional features for your critter on scrap paper in the colors of your choice. You might draw a nose, mouth, eyes, and whiskers. Cut out each piece and glue it onto the critter.

One Step More

Create other critters using various sizes of a different kind of shape, such as a circle or oval.

other examples:

Language Arts Link

Tell children that *crescent* and *critter* begin with the blend *cr.* Ask them to brainstorm other words that begin with *cr*, such as *crash, creek, crib, crop,* and *crunch.* List their responses on chart paper. Then, have children use words from the list to make up a story about a crazy critter. Have them write and illustrate their stories on half-sheets of paper and then bind the pages into a booklet. Later, challenge more advanced children to sort the one-syllable words from the list by vowel types (such as long and short vowels) and then by specific vowel sounds.

Related Reading

Have You Seen My Cat? by Eric Carle (Simon & Schuster, 1991)

Sea Shapes by Suse MacDonald (Voyager Books, 1998)

Three Pigs, One Wolf, Seven Magic Shapes by Grace Maccarone (Cartwheel, 1998)

Wavy Sea Animals

Use these colorful projects to reinforce children's knowledge of ocean animals or the properties of water.

Art Concepts
shape
color
pattern

Materials

To display:
- pictures of ocean animals (see Related Reading for books featuring ocean animal pictures)
- completed project

For each child:
- 4- by 6-inch construction paper in a light color
- pencil
- black marker
- scissors

To share:
- 10 sheets of yellow, blue, orange, and green construction paper in each of these sizes: 5- by 7-inch, 6- by 8-inch, 7- by 9-inch, and 8- by 10-inch
- glue sticks

Let's Begin

Display the ocean animal pictures. Discuss with children the different kinds of animals and their shapes. Then, show them the completed project. What ocean animal does the project resemble? Ask children to name the colors that surround the center shape. Show them how each color repeats the shape of the center figure, but is larger in size. This repeated shape creates a pattern. It also gives a wavy, ripple effect to the project, similar to the wavy lines that appear around an animal that moves in water.

Tell children that they will create a wavy sea animal of their choice. Pass out the materials, then demonstrate the procedures as children follow along.

Timesaving Tip!

Use a paper cutter to cut the construction paper in the sizes needed for the project. You can stack and cut several sheets of paper at a time.

Step by Step

1. Use pencil to draw the ocean animal of your choice onto the 4-by 6-inch light paper. Start by drawing a simple outline of the animal, making it as large as possible. Add just a few details to make the animal recognizable. Use the black marker to trace the details. Then, cut out the animal shape.

2. Choose a 5- by 7-inch sheet of paper in the color of your choice. Glue the animal cutout to the center of the paper. Use pencil to trace about ½- to ¾-inch away from the animal outline. Cut out the shape.

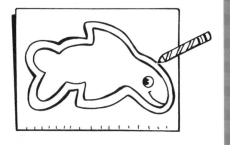

3. Glue the shape from Step 2 onto a sheet of 6- by 8-inch paper in a different color. Again, trace about ½- to ¾-inch away from the larger shape and cut out. Repeat this step two more times, each time using the next larger size paper in a color not yet used.

One Step More

Display the projects on a bulletin board covered with dark blue paper. Attach cutouts of coral, plants, and other ocean objects to create an underwater scene.

Language Arts Link

Tell children that an animal creates waves when it swims. Write *swim* on chart paper, say the word, and point out the beginning blend. Ask children to brainstorm other *sw* words, such as *swamp, swing,* and *swoosh* to add to the chart. Then, invite them to play "Sit or Swim." Explain that if you call out a word that begins with *sw*, they will get up and "swim" around the room. If the word does not begin with *sw*, they will sit down. Ask more advanced children to list the *sw* words they come across in their reading materials. Then, have them use as many of the words as possible to write a story about a real or imaginary sea animal.

Related Reading

Sea Critters by Sylvia Earle (National Geographic Children's Books, 2000)

Simon & Schuster Children's Guide to Sea Creatures by Jinny Johnson (Simon & Schuster, 1998)

A Swim Through the Sea by Kristin Joy Pratt (Dawn Publications, 1994)

3-D Animal Habitats

Invite children to use these three-dimensional projects to share their knowledge of animals and their habitats.

Art Concepts
shape
two-dimensional
three-dimensional

Materials

To display:
- pictures of animals in different kinds of habitats (see Related Reading for books featuring pictures of animals in their habitats)
- completed project

For each child:
- 9- by 12-inch heavy tagboard
- pencil
- black marker
- color markers including brown and gray
- air-drying clay (or modeling compound) in the size of a ping-pong ball

To share:
- glue sticks
- raffia
- green crepe paper strips
- craft sticks
- toothpicks, yarn, and pipe cleaners
- white glue

Let's Begin

Display the pictures of animals in their habitats and the completed project. Discuss what kinds of animals and things are found in each of the pictured habitats. Then, talk about the habitat represented by the completed project. Ask children to point out some of the shapes used to create the habitat. Afterward, explain that a shape, such as paper, has only two-dimensions—width and height. When the shape is formed so that it has width, height, and depth, it becomes a three-dimensional object. Finally, invite volunteers to point out and describe the two-dimensional and three-dimensional elements in the project.

Tell children that they will create an animal habitat of their choice, such as a cave, river, pond, rain forest, ocean, jungle, grassland, desert, and so on. Pass out the materials. Then, demonstrate the procedures as children follow along.

Timesaving Tip!

Separate the modeling compound ahead of time, store each clay ball in a resealable plastic bag, and then distribute the bags when ready to use.

Step by Step

1. Fold the tagboard in half horizontally. Unfold the tagboard and place it vertically on the table.

2. Decide what habitat to create. Use pencil to draw the ground of the habitat on the bottom half of the tagboard. For a forest, you might include rocks, leaves, and logs. For the ocean, you might draw coral, plants, and shells. Be sure to include only things that would be found in the habitat.

3. On the top half of the tagboard, draw things that might be found above the ground in the habitat. For a forest, you might include trees and clouds. For the ocean, you might draw rock formations and ocean animals.

4. Trace all the drawings with the black marker and then color them with color markers. If desired, glue raffia or green crepe paper strips onto the habitat to give the appearance of grass, leaves, or other objects.

5. Create from the modeling clay one or more animals that live in the habitat. Use a craft stick to add texture and draw facial features on each animal. If desired, use toothpicks, yarn, or pipe cleaners to make limbs, antennae, or other features. Set each animal aside to dry. This might take several days to a week, depending on the thickness of the patty, the humidity, and room temperature.

6. Color each animal with color markers. Then, use white glue to glue it onto the habitat.

7. Fold up the top half of the habitat and display it on a flat surface against a wall.

One Step More

To make a stand for the habitat, fan-fold a 2½- by 8-inch strip of heavy tagboard into sixths. Glue one end to the top back of the habitat, then extend the strip in stair-step fashion to form a stand.

Language Arts Link

Write *home* on the chalkboard. Ask children to say the word and tell what vowel sound they hear. Have them name other words that contain the long o sound, such as *bone, hole, joke, rode,* and *vote*. Write their responses on the board. Afterward, have volunteers underline each long o word that is spelled with the CVCe pattern. Then, invite children to use these words to create songs about home. They might set their songs to the tune of a familiar song or chant. Ask more advanced children to write their songs on a large sheet of paper. Then, have them point to the words as a small group sings along.

Related Reading

All Kinds of Habitats by Sally Hewitt (Children's Press, 1999)

Animals in Their Habitats series by Francine Galko (Heinemann, 2002)

I See a Kookaburra!: Discovering Animal Habitats Around the World by Robin Page (Houghton Mifflin, 2005)

The Magic School Bus Hops Home: A Book About Animal Habitats by Pat Relf (Scholastic, 1995)

In the Style of Piet Mondrian: Bold Geometric Paintings

Reinforce geometric shapes, measurement, and size with these bold Mondrian-inspired paintings.

Art Concepts

line
shape
color

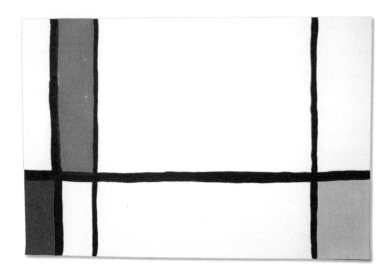

Let's Begin

Show children *Composition with Red, Blue, and Yellow, 1930.* Tell them that the artist, Piet Mondrian, was famous for abstract paintings such as this one. Ask them to name the kind of lines seen in the painting. Then, explain that Mondrian used horizontal and vertical lines and angles to create his work. What shapes do the lines and angles form? Are the shapes all the same size? Point out how the artist filled each shape with a primary color (red, yellow, and blue) or white and then used black lines of different thicknesses to outline the shapes. Finally, show children the completed project. Have them compare the lines, shapes, and colors to the Mondrian painting.

Tell children that they will create Mondrian-style paintings. Pass out the materials and demonstrate the procedures as children follow along.

Materials

To display:

- *Composition with Red, Blue, and Yellow, 1930,* by Piet Mondrian (page 207)
- completed project

For each child:

- 12- by 18-inch white construction paper
- pencil
- ruler
- yellow chalk

For paint stations:

- five containers each of black, red, yellow, and blue tempera paint
- 25 paintbrushes

Timesaving Tip!

Set up the paint stations ahead of time. Cover four tables with newspaper and place five paintbrushes on each one. Just before beginning the activity, place a different paint color on each table.

Step by Step

1. Using the pencil and ruler, lightly draw horizontal and vertical lines to create an assortment of squares and rectangles on the white paper. Draw the shapes in different sizes and make sure the lines of each shape are shared with other shapes.

2. Decide which shapes you want to paint and what colors to use. Then, using chalk, lightly write in each shape the first letter of the color you've chosen to paint it: R for red, B for blue, and Y for yellow. Don't write anything in the shapes that you've decided to leave white.

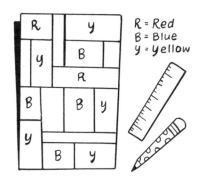

3. Take the drawing to the paint stations. Paint each shape with the selected color. Paint all the shapes in one color before moving to the next color.

4. When the shapes dry, paint all the lines of the shapes with black paint. To add interest, vary the thickness of the lines so that some shapes have thin lines and others have thick lines.

One Step More

Mount all the paintings on a bulletin board covered with black paper. Title the display "Mondrian-Style Masterpieces."

Language Arts Link

Write *square* and *rectangle* on chart paper. Remind children that Mondrian often used these shapes in his art. Then, have children name other shapes to add to the chart. After reviewing the words, ask children to draw and cut out five large shapes of their choice. Have them write the name of each shape on the corresponding cutout and add a drawing of something that has the same shape. Finally, have them glue their cutouts onto construction paper to create a shape collage. Invite more advanced children to add a written description of each shape to their collage.

Related Reading

The Greedy Triangle by Marilyn Burns (Scholastic, 1995)

I Spy Shapes in Art by Lucy Micklethwait (Greenwillow, 2004)

Mouse Paint by Ellen Stoll Walsh (Harcourt Children's Books, 1989)

When a Line Bends...A Shape Begins by Rhonda Gowler Greene (Houghton Mifflin, 2001)

School Bus Pattern

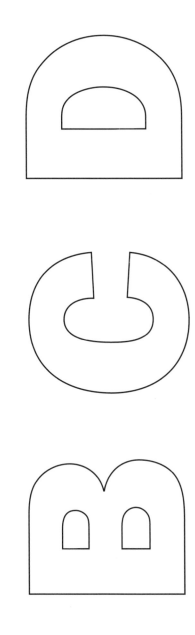
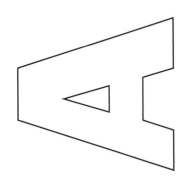
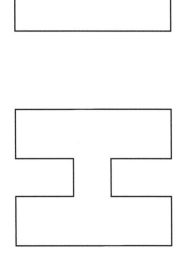
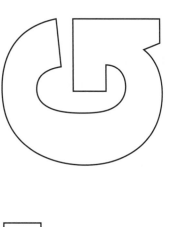
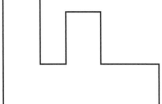
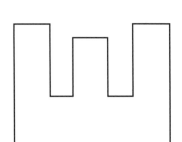
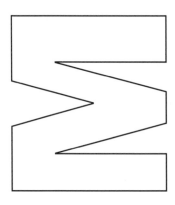
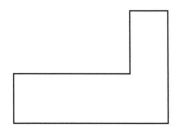
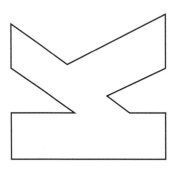
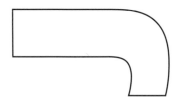

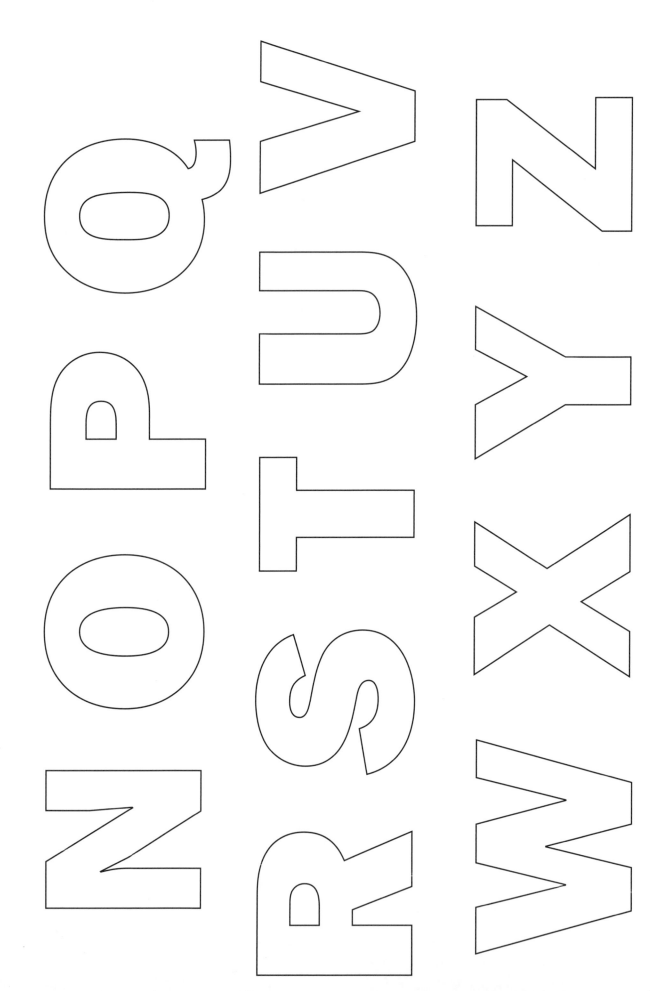

The Big Book of Quick & Easy Art Activities   Scholastic Teaching Resources

Shape Patterns

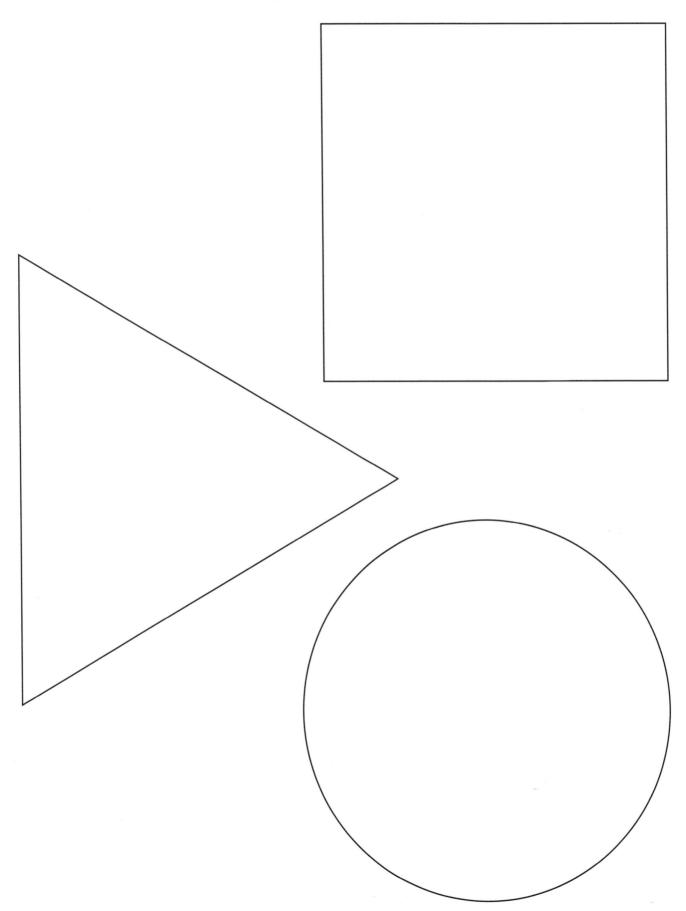

Leaf Patterns

Pumpkin Pattern

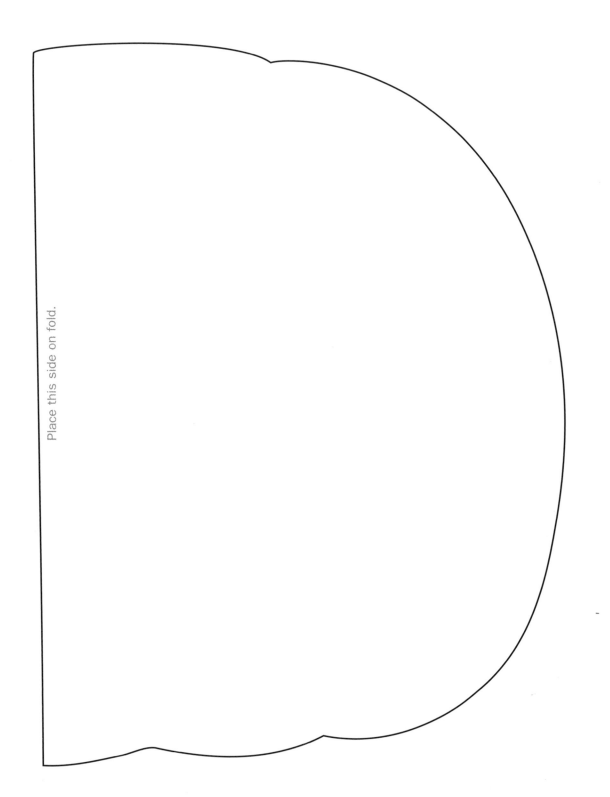

Place this side on fold.

Turkey Pattern

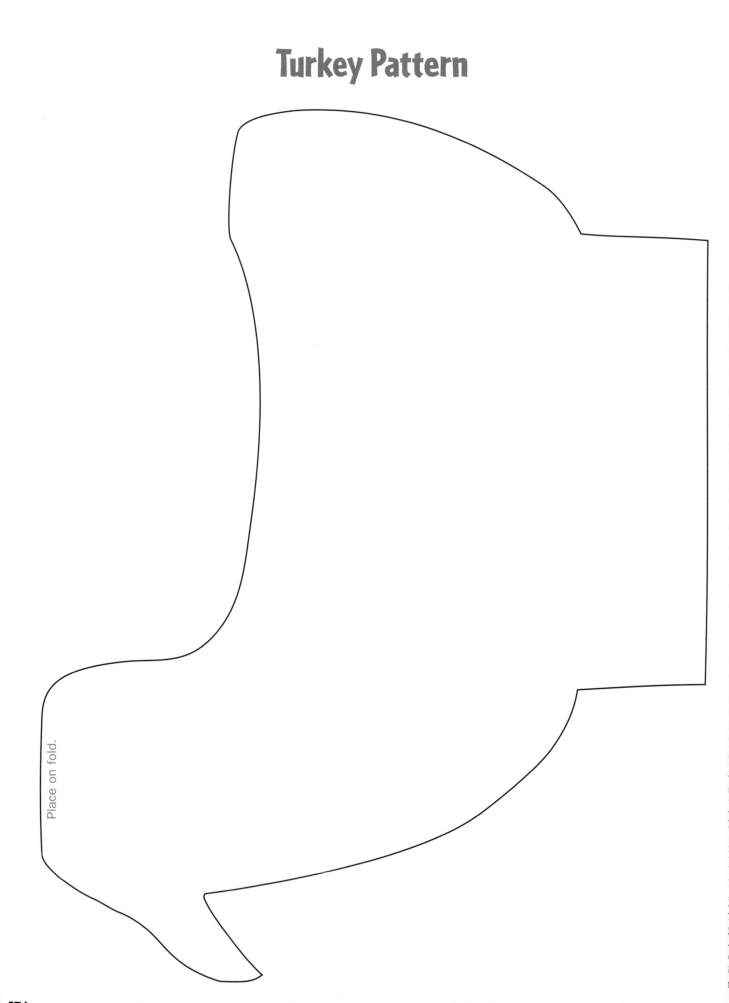

Place on fold.

The Big Book of Quick & Easy Art Activities Scholastic Teaching Resources

Stocking Pattern

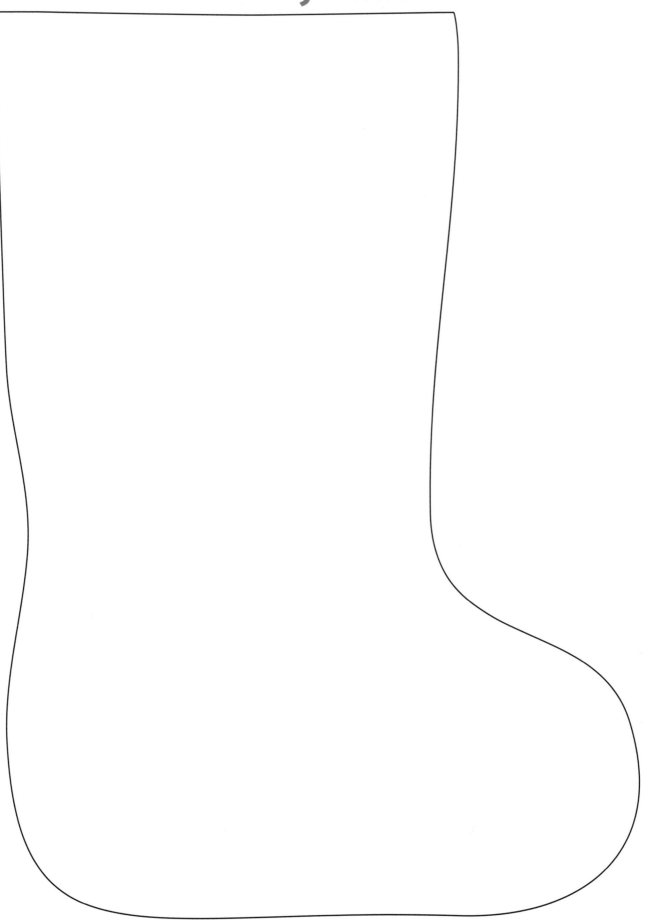

Kwanzaa Shapes

Watch Face and Hand Patterns

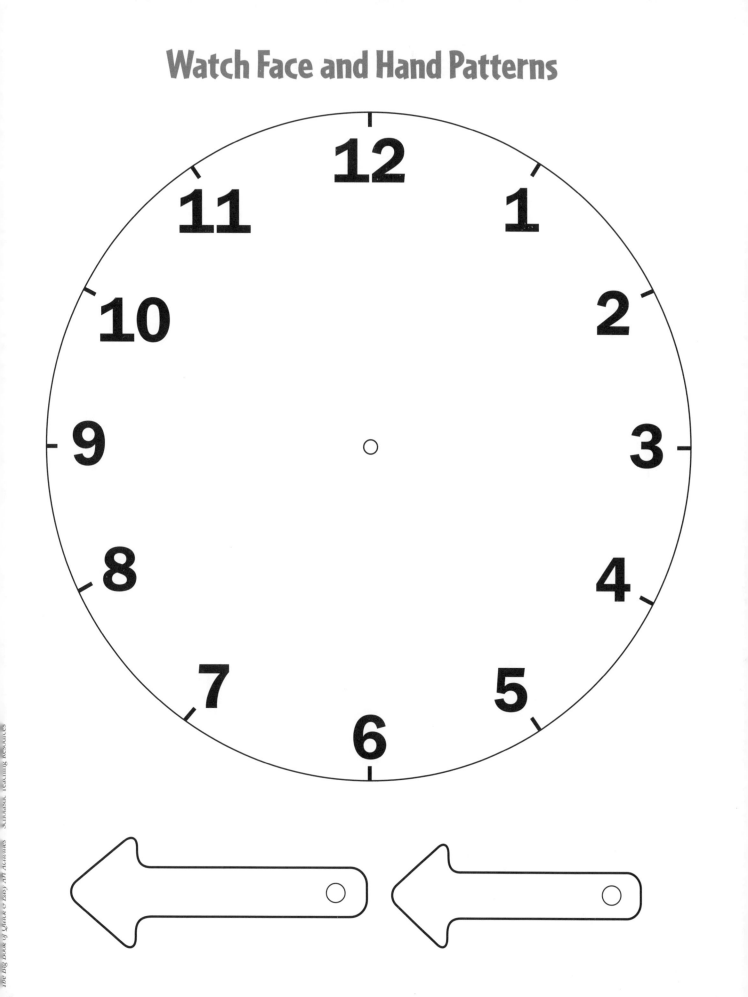

Jacket Pattern

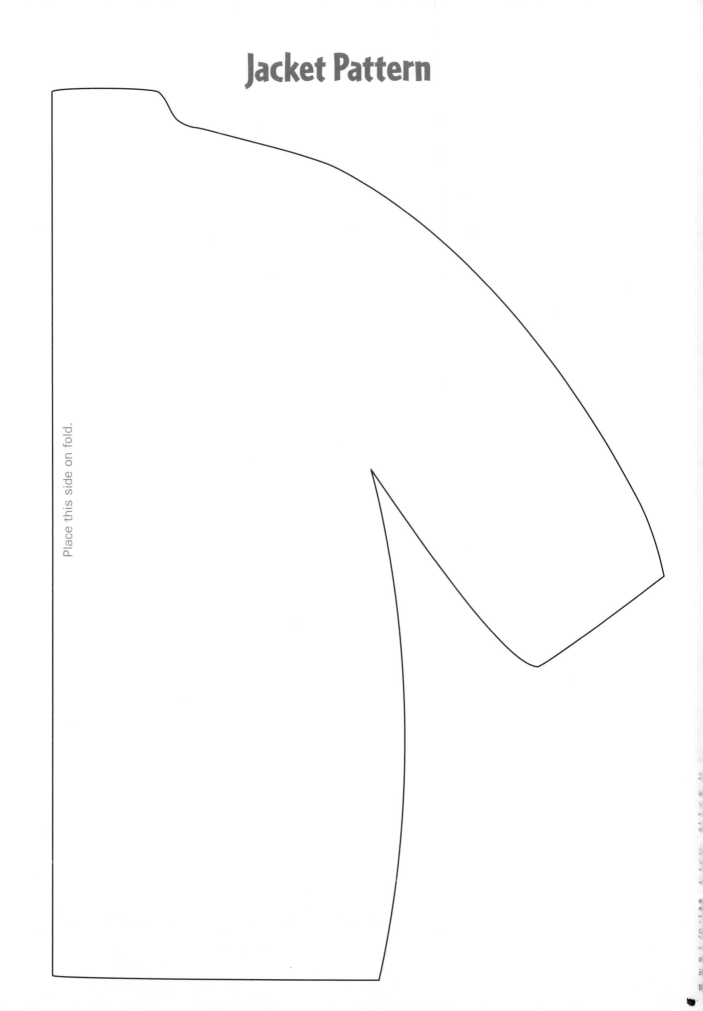

Place this side on fold.

Mitten Pattern

Bear Puppet Patterns

paw

ear

Lion and Lamb Patterns

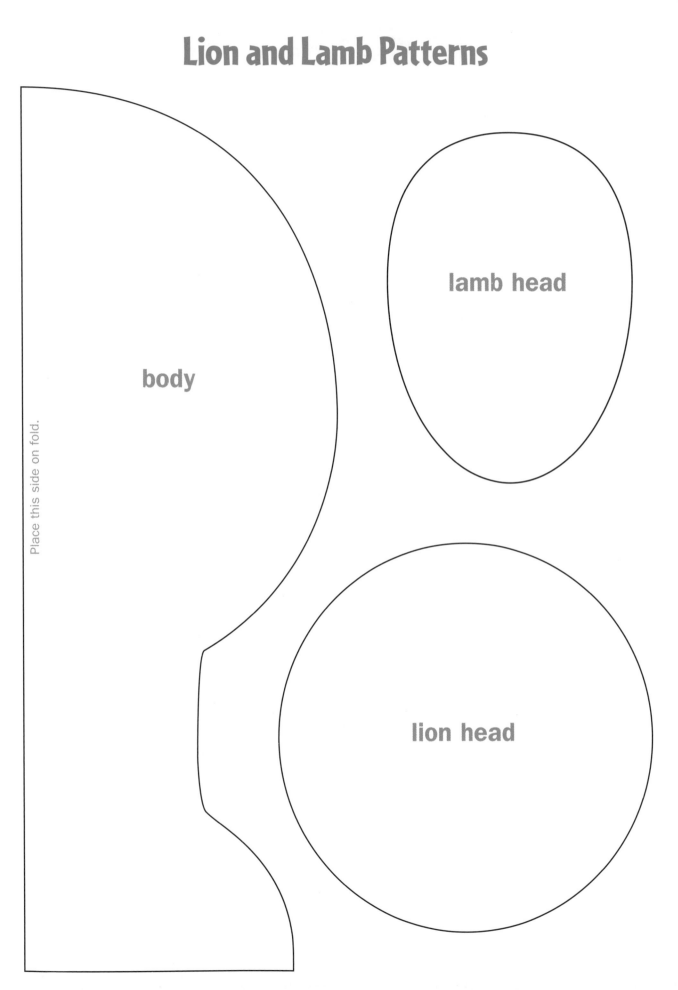

Place this side on fold.

body

lamb head

lion head

Kite Pattern

Leprechaun Patterns

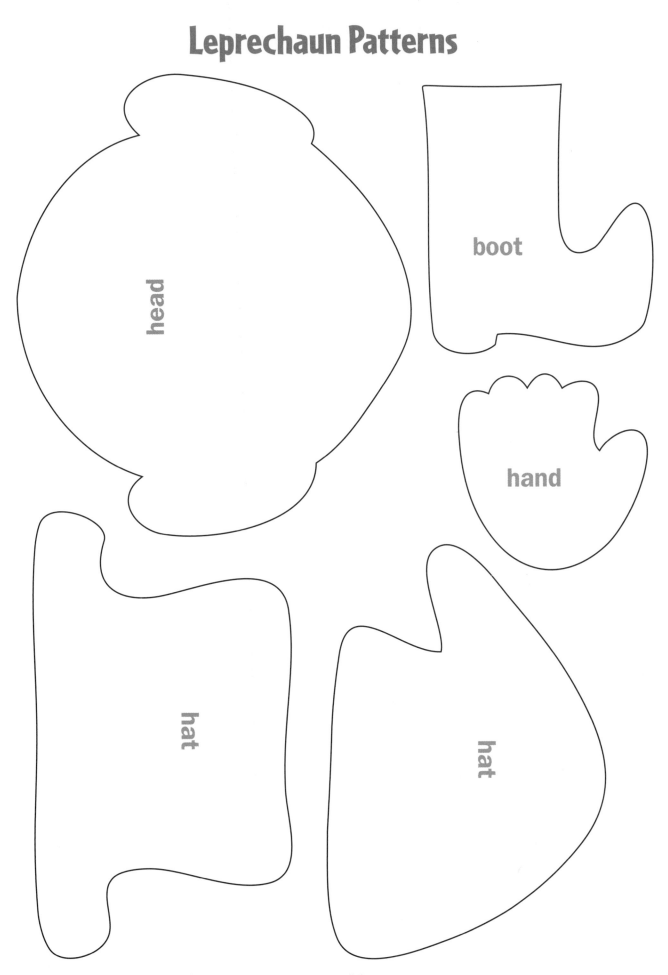

head

boot

hand

hat

hat

Parrot Patterns

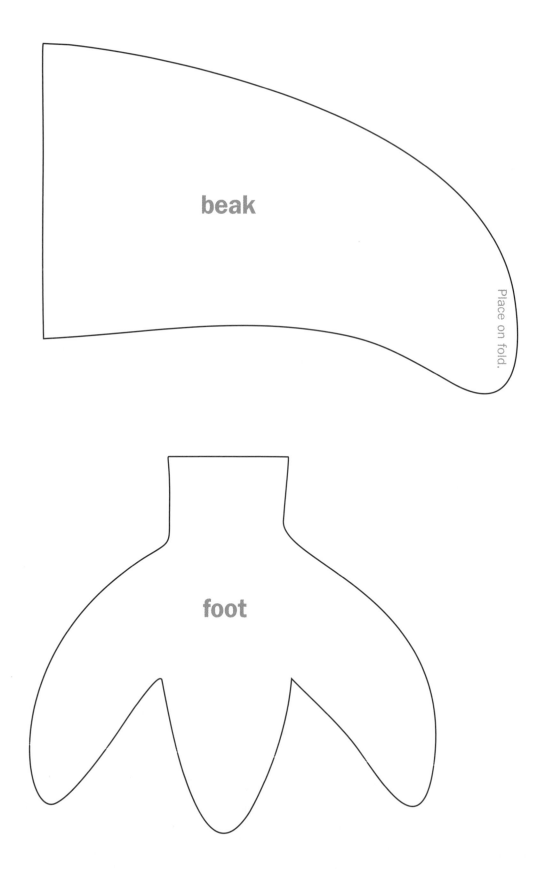

beak

Place on fold.

foot

Rabbit and Hat Patterns

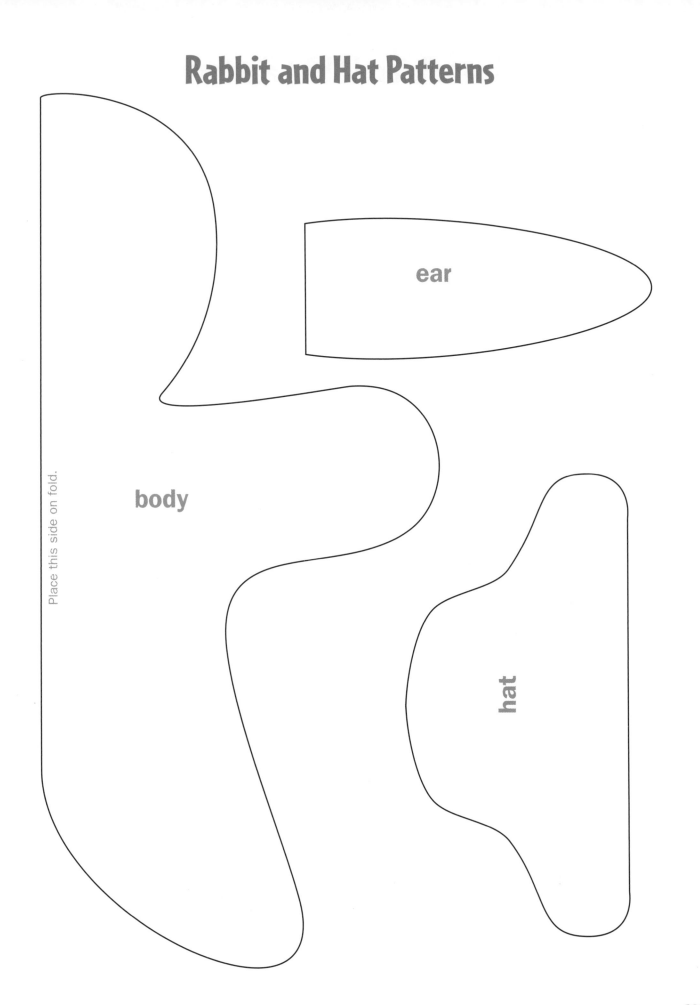

Place this side on fold.

ear

body

hat

Overalls and Shirt Patterns

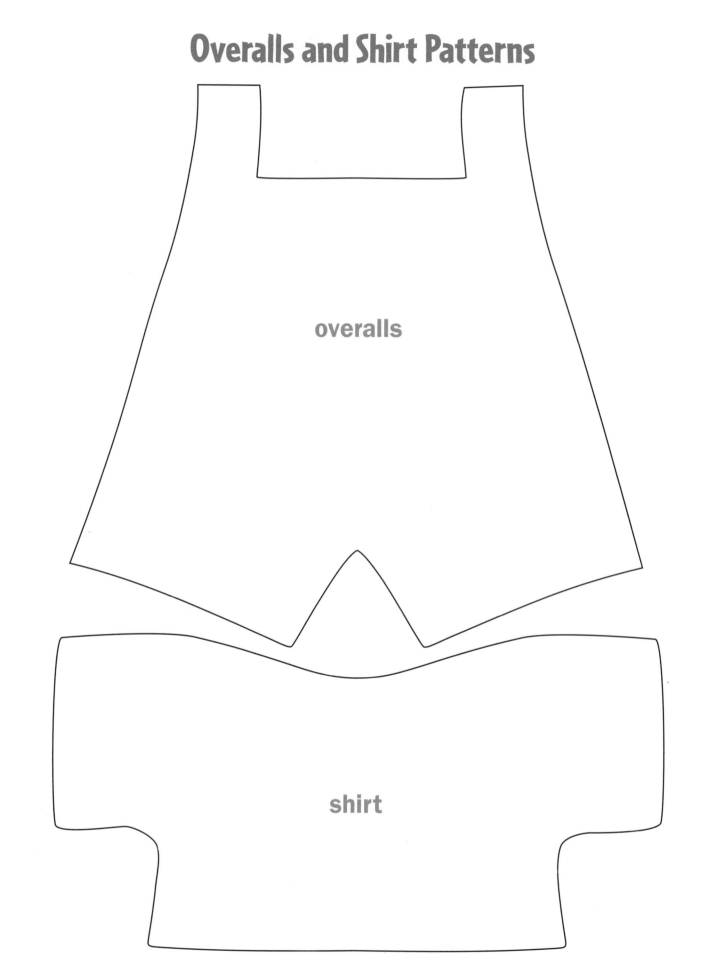

overalls

shirt

Butterfly Pattern

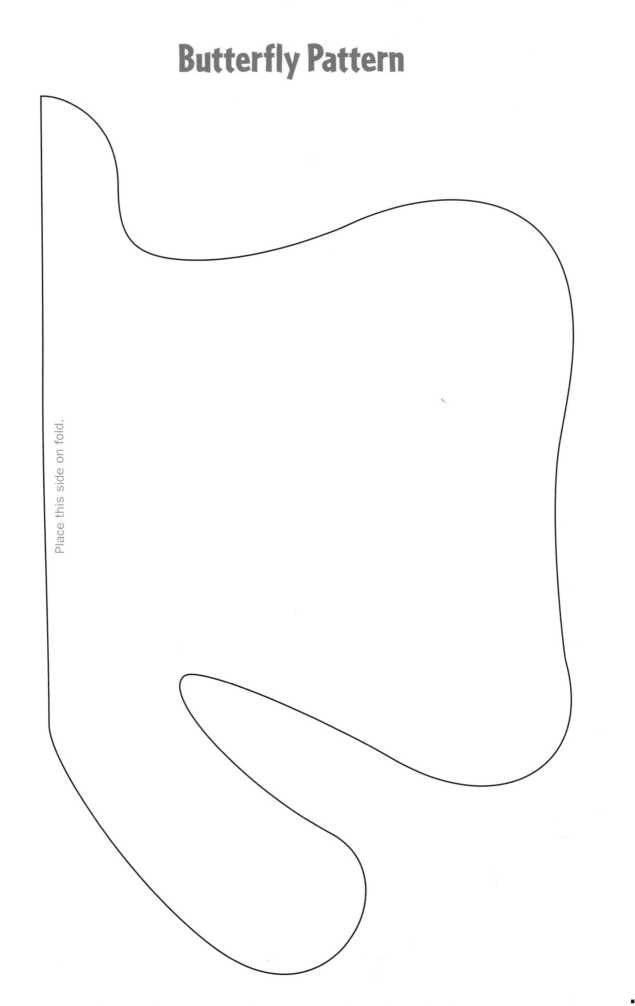

Place this side on fold.

Sneaker Patterns

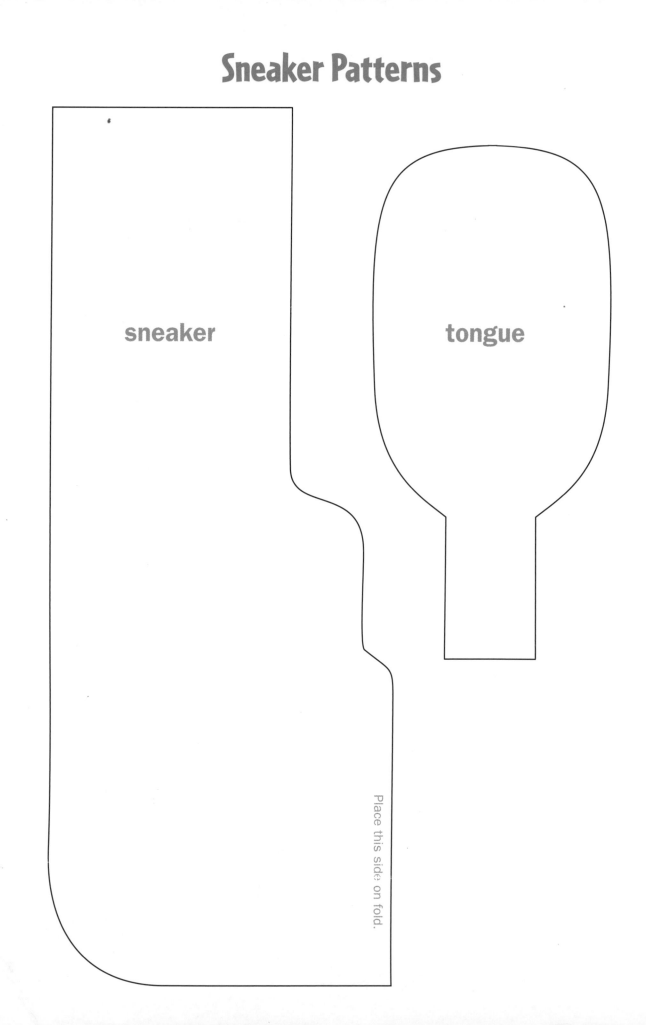

sneaker

tongue

Place this side on fold.

The Big Book of Quick & Easy Art Activities   Scholastic Teaching Resources

Sunflower Pattern

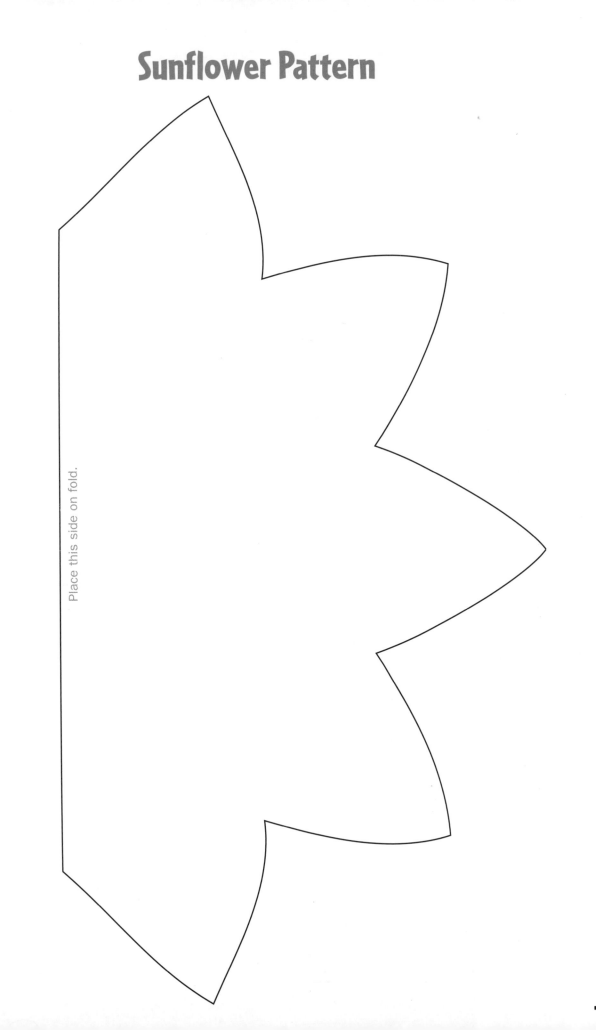

Place this side on fold.

Sunglasses Patterns

The Big Book of Quick & Easy Art Activities   Scholastic Teaching Resources

Sun Visor Pattern

Flip-Flop Pattern

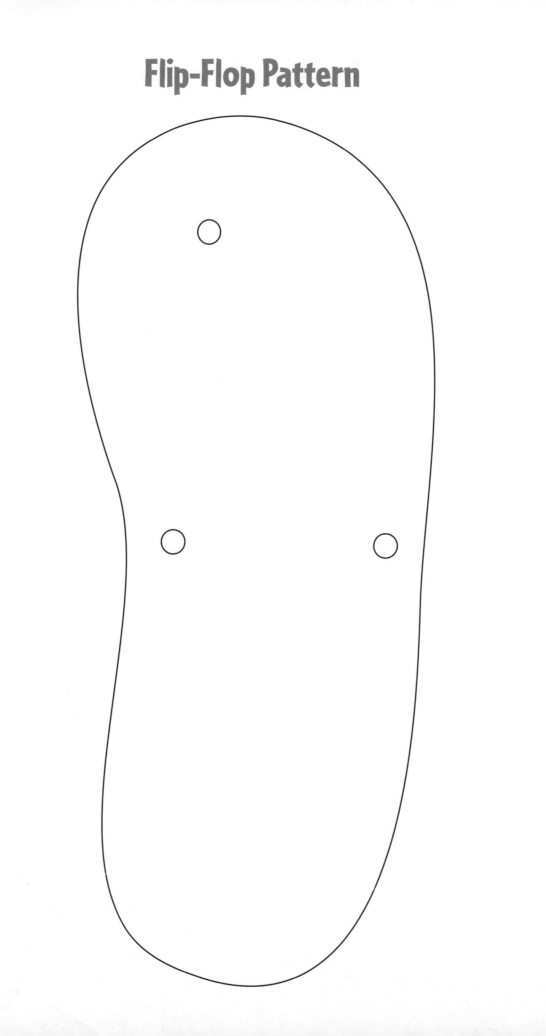

The Big Book of Quick & Easy Art Activities · Scholastic Teaching Resources

Fishbowl Pattern

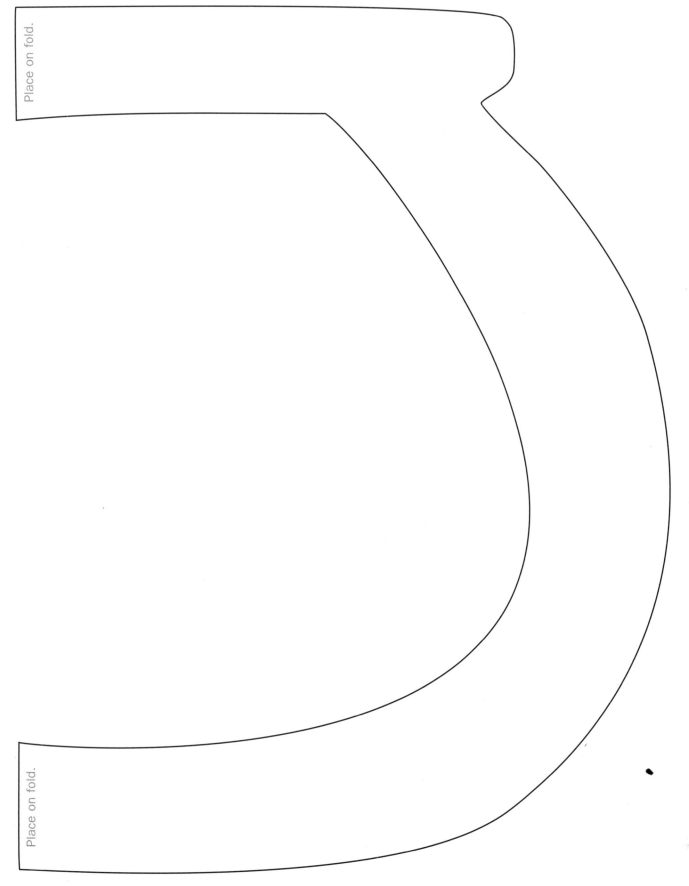

Place on fold.

Place on fold.

Stretchin' Uncle Sam Pattern

Elephant Puzzle Pattern

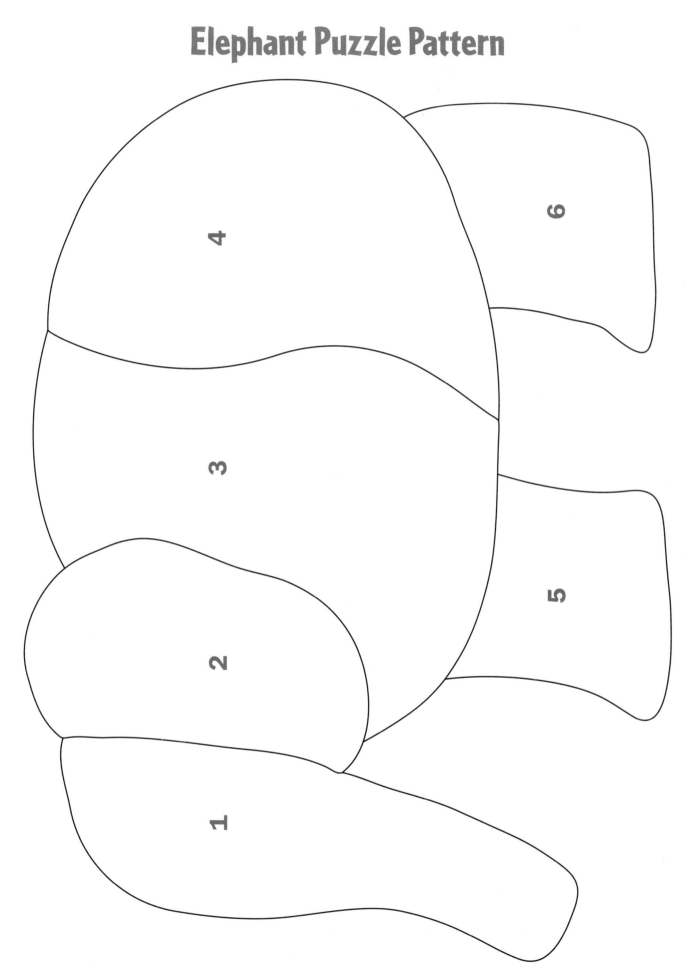

Crescent Shape Patterns

Color Wheel

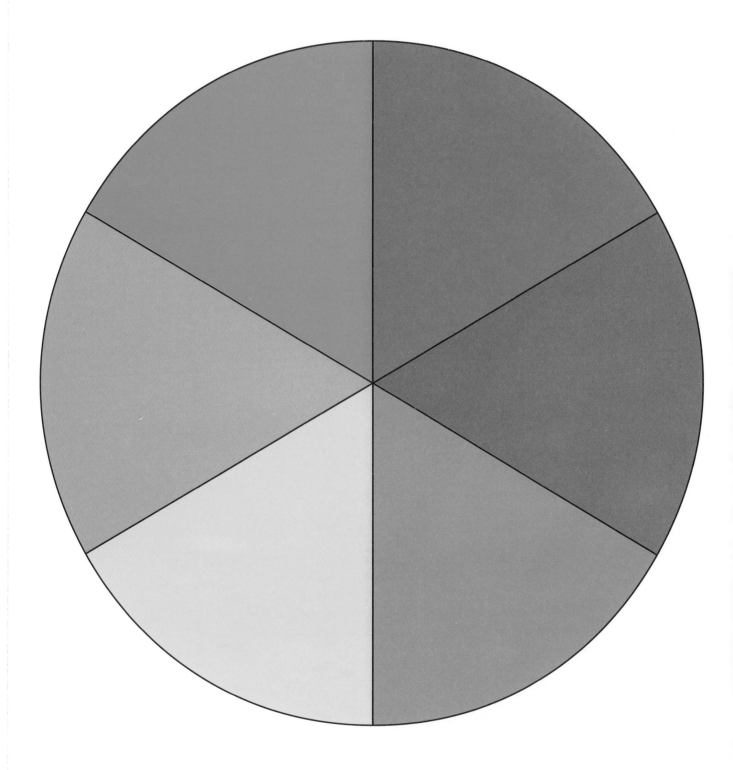

Texture Reference Chart

Symmetry E118 by M.C. Escher

M.C. Escher's "Symmetry Drawing E118" © 2006 The M.C.Escher Company-Holland. All rights reserved.

Starry Night by Vincent Van Gogh

Les Vegetaux
by Henri Matisse

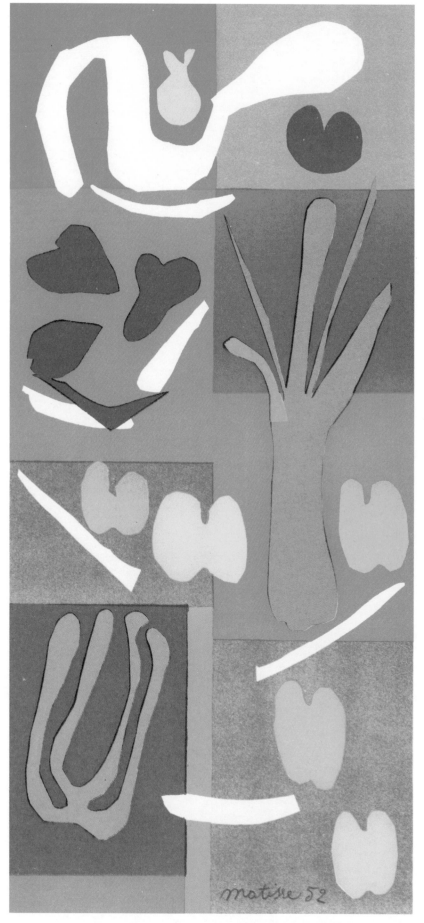

matisse 52

Composition with Red, Blue, and Yellow, 1930
by Piet Mondrian

Composition with Red, Blue and Yellow, 1930
Oil on canvas, 46 x 46 cm
© 2007 Mondrian/Holtzman Trust
c/o HCR International, Warrenton, VA